MW00379264

The Quakers

*A Captivating Guide to a Historically
Christian Group and How William Penn
Founded the Colony of Pennsylvania in
British North America*

© Copyright 2019

All Rights Reserved. No part of this book may be reproduced in any form without permission in writing from the author. Reviewers may quote brief passages in reviews.

Disclaimer: No part of this publication may be reproduced or transmitted in any form or by any means, mechanical or electronic, including photocopying or recording, or by any information storage and retrieval system, or transmitted by email without permission in writing from the publisher.

While all attempts have been made to verify the information provided in this publication, neither the author nor the publisher assumes any responsibility for errors, omissions or contrary interpretations of the subject matter herein.

This book is for entertainment purposes only. The views expressed are those of the author alone, and should not be taken as expert instruction or commands. The reader is responsible for his or her own actions.

Adherence to all applicable laws and regulations, including international, federal, state and local laws governing professional licensing, business practices, advertising and all other aspects of doing business in the US, Canada, UK or any other jurisdiction is the sole responsibility of the purchaser or reader.

Neither the author nor the publisher assumes any responsibility or liability whatsoever on the behalf of the purchaser or reader of these materials. Any perceived slight of any individual or organization is purely unintentional.

Free Bonus from Captivating History (Available for a Limited time)

Hi History Lovers!

Now you have a chance to join our exclusive history list so you can get your first history ebook for free as well as discounts and a potential to get more history books for free! Simply visit the link below to join.

Captivatinghistory.com/ebook

Also, make sure to follow us on Facebook, Twitter and Youtube by searching for Captivating History.

Contents

Introduction: The Origins of the Quakers

The Quakers, known for their austere religious beliefs and strong social convictions, were very much a product of the English Civil War. It's important to note that the "English Civil War" was a series of three large uprisings against English governance that took place between 1642 and 1651. The origins of this upheaval can be traced back even further, to the year 1625.

For it was in 1625 that Charles the First came to the throne in England, and he brought considerable discord to the kingdom. Much of this discord had to do with religion and state. Charles didn't feel that he should be questioned by Parliament since he believed he had a God-given right to reign over his people. But ever since the signing of the Magna Carter in 1215, which limited the English monarch's power, the days of absolute authority over the kingdom had long since passed.

By 1640, King Charles had developed an increasingly antagonistic relationship with the British Parliament. Charles was fed up with members of Parliament, whom he viewed as obstructionists to his policy, and he was also irked at what he felt was longstanding resentment for his choice of marrying a woman of Spanish Catholic background. England had become increasingly Protestant, and a virulent strain of anti-Catholic sentiment ran rampant throughout the British Isles.

King Charles was attempting to put down a rebellion in Scotland at the time, but he needed members of Parliament to approve the taxation required to raise money for the enterprise. Parliament dithered and began to insist that King Charles further limit the scope of his authority. For a king like Charles, who believed that it was God's will for him to rule, this, of course, did not sit well. He lost his patience and tried to have some of his opposition arrested instead.

These Parliament members were notified ahead of time and managed to make a break for it before the king could put them in irons. Shortly after, two factions rose—one loyal to the king and the other loyal to Parliament—and faced off against each other. English society was about as fractured as possible, with regular citizens and the military splintering into the two sides.

While the British factions of the Parliamentarians and Royalists battled it out over just what kind of constitution and governance Great Britain was going to have, another argument was taking place in religious circles. Previously, the Church of England had dominated all religious affairs, but with the iron-fisted monarchy's downfall, England's first real religious reformation took shape.

It was out of this tumult that the Quakers were born. The first Quakers can be traced back to the East Midlands of England. And the first well-documented instance of Quaker happenings seems to have occurred in 1647. For it was that year that a Quaker firebrand by the name of George Fox came into his own. George Fox was one of the many individuals who became disillusioned with the official doctrine of the Church of England during this period.

Fox also allegedly had some visionary experiences in which he was persuaded that a "direct experience of Christ" outside of the official doctrine of the Church of England could be achieved. Taking his beliefs to the people, Fox began to preach his message all over

England, as well as in Holland and even as far as Barbados, which was a British colony at the time. For his efforts, Fox was eventually arrested and made to answer charges of "religious blasphemy."

It was during his interrogation by authorities that George Fox quoted scripture from the Book of Isaiah and advised his accusers to fear God and "tremble and quake at the word of the Lord." Fox was roundly ridiculed for his words and was subsequently dubbed a "Quaker" for this advice. The term began as a pejorative against the movement's leader, but Fox's followers soon embraced the term and made it their own. They would later rebrand themselves as the "Society of Friends," but the moniker of "Quaker" would remain their ultimate calling card.

By early 1652, the group had gained significant momentum and had acquired some powerful emissaries in the form of James Nayler and Richard Farnsworth. Richard Farnsworth would become Fox's right-hand man when it came to evangelism. However, Fox parted company with Farnsworth in the summer of 1652, for this was the year Fox engaged in a renewed campaign across northern England. He was a tireless evangelist, and even when he was "pelted with stones on Walney Island," a region off the west coast of England, in September of 1652, he faithfully soldiered on.

In 1654, after spending two years roaming the countryside, Fox made his way to London, where he was ready to spread the Quaker faith to those that flocked to the city. The faith would greatly expand from here, and as a result of the many ministrations of Fox and his friends, by the end of the decade, the Quakers numbered in the tens of thousands. However, as their popularity grew, so did their persecution.

Many other mainline Christians viewed the Quakers as a dangerous sect, so much so that they pressured the British Parliament to pass the Quaker Act of 1662. This act set forth in law the "prescribed form" of prayer and worship as designated by the state. It was a formula that specifically left the traditions of the Quakers out.

Unable to gain acceptance in England, the Quakers would soon leave the place of their origin altogether and try their luck in a brave new world on another continent.

Chapter 1: The Quakers Arrive in America

The Lord showed me, so that I did see clearly, that he did not dwell in these temples which men had commanded and set up, but in people's hearts. His people were his temple, and he dwelt in them.

–George Fox

The first wave of Quakers reached America in the 1650s. The first documented arrival of a Quaker in America was a woman by the name of Elizabeth Harris, who arrived in the Chesapeake Bay area around the year 1655. It's said that she had "left her husband and son behind in England" in order to "evangelize the Puritan remnant" that remained in the region. This outreach was not always something the Puritans would take too kindly to. As the years passed, these two religious worlds would continue to collide, as one would try to convince the other of their ideological superiority. And in this struggle, it must be said that it was the Puritans who bared their teeth.

While the Quakers sought to persuade their Puritan neighbors with their preaching, the Puritans sought to curtail the Quakers through sheer force. There is a reason why the phrase "puritanical" has come to refer to someone or something that is unbending in their beliefs.

Ironically, the Puritans were initially persecuted back in England for breaking away from the Anglican faith. Yet as soon as they reached the New World and set up their own little puritanical enclaves, the persecuted Puritans quickly became the persecutors. They attempted to stamp out any beliefs that they had come to view as being "heretical" to their particular brand of Christianity.

However, early American Quakers, like Elizabeth Harris, were not going to be steamrolled by the Puritans quite so easily. Harris turned out to be a rather convincing evangelist, and despite any puritanical oppression sent her way, she developed many strong converts. She even managed to persuade a notable man of the community by the name of Thomas Marsh to join the Quakers, who, in turn, brought his entire family into the religion's fold, creating a bastion of Quakers on their little settlement of Marsh's Seat. But perhaps the most significant of her converts was William Fuller, who was a member of the governor's council in Maryland. It was this conversion of prominent members of the community that created a backlash against the nascent Quaker community.

In 1656, while Elizabeth Harris was having much success in evangelizing to the locals, two new Quakers arrived from Britain and began to try their luck. They were Mary Fisher and Ann Austin. These two ladies preached all over Massachusetts, hoping to win hearts and minds over to Quakerism, but the prevailing authority figures of Boston, Massachusetts, shut them down rather quickly.

The women were taken into custody for their efforts. They had their "Quaker books" burned and were closely examined to see if they showed any signs of being witches. After all, this was Massachusetts, the colony in which the infamous Salem witch trials would take place between 1692 and 1693. The idea that someone was a witch and working for the evil one was no laughing matter for the Puritans, and almost anyone preaching a different doctrine than what they were used to was immediately suspect.

It's unclear whether they believed the women were witches or not, but shortly thereafter, they were both shipped off to Barbados—an island in the Caribbean—seemingly banished to the most remote British settlement in the Western Hemisphere at that time. Soon, the provincial legislature even went so far as to pass a law refusing to allow Quakers access to their territory. They also fined ship captains who had the audacity of simply bringing a proselytizing Quaker to their shores.

New converts among the colonists were equally mistreated. If a fellow neighbor found out about one's conversion to Quakerism, they faced having their land taken from them and being exiled from the community. Sometimes even their children were at risk of being confiscated. In one instance, a couple of Quaker kids were threatened with banishment to Barbados, where they would be forced into indentured servitude. The only reason this punishment wasn't meted out was simply that the colonial authorities were unable to procure a ship willing to do their bidding. As all of these draconian measures taken by colonial leadership would seem to indicate, the Quakers were now officially *persona non grata*. And by 1660, the same persecution the Quakers had left behind in England came home to roost in the British colonies of Maryland and Massachusetts, this time with a vengeance.

It was in Massachusetts that the Quaker evangelist Mary Dyer was given a death sentence for her faith. On June 1ˢᵗ, 1660, she was executed on the authority of the Bostonian government for daring to proselytize in Boston. Right before she was executed, Mary was told that she would be set free if she simply gave her word that she would leave and never return.

There were two problems with this request. Number one, Quakers don't swear to do anything, and number two, Mary Dyer would rather die than give up preaching to the folks of Massachusetts. She readily replied, "Nay, I cannot, for in obedience to the will of the Lord God I came, and in his will I abide faithful to death." Even in death, Mary would manage to send shockwaves throughout the colonies, bringing greater attention to Quakerism than if she had simply been left to preach in peace.

So much so that, in 1661, this action would eventually provoke a response from none other than the king of England, Charles II, who, in a sudden show of compassion, made it expressly forbidden for anyone in the Massachusetts Bay Colony to hand out death penalties to those "professing Quakerism." Nevertheless, despite efforts to enforce toleration, non-Quakers often viewed Quakers with absolute contempt. Quakers were roundly criticized for their refusal to show deference to authority figures, as well as for having religious beliefs that others in the community felt were heretical.

Meanwhile, back in England, George Fox and his fellow British Friends began to use Britain's legal law to further ensure their freedom of religion. This was done through appeals and pointing out loopholes in the law as it pertained to the cases of Quakers who had been imprisoned. Quakers would even seek audiences with the king himself, so they could request pardons for those Quakers being detained.

Even though more tolerant measures had been achieved, there was still great suspicion in British society that the Quakers were an alien presence among them. British society had already undergone many upheavals in recent years, and it didn't take much for fringe groups, such as the Quakers, to be perceived as a potential threat to the social order. It was for this reason that George Fox wrote down his famous "Peace Testimony" in 1661.

This epic testimony laid out the Quaker intention to live peaceably with their neighbors and sought to clear the Quaker name of any "accusations of plot and fighting and demonstrate their innocency [sic]." The testament then went on to state the following affirmation: "All bloody principles and practices, we do utterly deny, with all outward wars and strife and fightings [sic] with outward weapons, for any end or under any pretense whatsoever."

Not only did this document help to calm some British nerves, but it also set forth the prime directive and charter that the Quakers would follow in the centuries to come. Here in this treatise, George Fox made it absolutely clear to his followers that Quakers needed to be above the fray when it came to violence of any kind. If there was any doubt among the Society of Friends over whether or not pacifism would reign supreme, it was as good as written in stone now.

Pacifism wasn't the only thing the Quaker Peace Testimony enshrined. It also represented a turning point in Quakerism, as they were moving away from the more radical Quaker past. Previously, the Quakers, galvanized by a younger George Fox, had enthusiastically preached of the imminent arrival of the end times. And like any religious group thinking the end was near, they sought to get their message across at all costs, even if it meant belligerently interrupting a service or two.

Yes, one of the oddest things about early Quakers was their penchant for bursting into the church of another denomination to proclaim their gospel while the Presbyterians, Methodists, Lutherans, Puritans—or whoever they might be—were in the middle of their sermon. This move certainly didn't gain Quakers very much sympathy from the leaders of other denominations, but this radical aspect of Quakerism seemed to suddenly come to an end with George Fox's Peace Testimony.

The Quakers who came after Fox's guidelines were laid out became much more pragmatic in their approach to ministry. Just like other religious sects that went from a cult-like status to becoming part of the mainstream, the Quakers moved away from a take-no-prisoners approach to a more organized outreach. They no longer expected an imminent Armageddon and instead focused on a long-term and strategic plan for evangelism.

It was during this period the Quakers first hammered out the official shape of their own religious gatherings. It was determined that the Quakers would meet on a "monthly, quarterly, and yearly" basis.

These gatherings would be referred to as "meetings." The concept of having monthly, quarterly, and yearly meetings is one that is still practiced among the faithful Quakers to this very day.

Back in the states, the Quakers continued to maintain a strong presence in southern Maryland, as well as Salem, Massachusetts. The Quakers were also present in the Dutch colony of New Netherland (later New York) as well. Quakers initially faced persecution from the Dutch, but by the early 1660s, the Dutch government ordered the people to leave the Quakers alone as long as "they remained peaceable." This policy was then continued by the British when they took over the colony in 1664.

Since this general acceptance continued, the founder of the Quaker faith, George Fox himself, set sail for the Americas on August 11th, 1671. Although it was styled as a grand tour, Fox was basically there to check the pulse of these satellites and make sure the various Quaker organizations were foundationally solid. Fox, along with his right-hand man, William Edmundson, first arrived at the Caribbean island of Barbados in October 1671.

It was here that Fox once again played the role of a Quaker apologist. Since tensions between the slaveholding populace and the Quakers of Barbados had begun to erupt, Fox fired off a letter to Colonel Christopher Codrington, the governor of the island, assuring him that the Quakers were not intentionally inciting slave rebellions. The animosity the plantation owners felt toward the Quakers was largely due to the fact that Quakers had made it their practice to preach to both the free and slave populations of the island.

Fox ended up meeting with the governor in person, and the meeting is said to have gone well, with Fox later reporting that "they were treated very civilly and kindly." Nevertheless, Fox refused to stop preaching and reaching out to the enslaved Africans on the island. While seeking to soothe the nerves of the island's governor, he instructed the Quaker faithful to continue to "take the enslaved to meetings to educate them." He also urged slave owners to "deal mildly and gently with them [slaves] and not use cruelty."

It wasn't long before the folks running the plantation began to complain that Fox and his Friends were "rabble-rousing." Fox soon left Barbados, and after a brief stint in Jamaica, he went to the mainland of what would become the United States, sailing all the way up to Maryland. As mentioned, the Quakers already had a strong presence in Maryland, and George Fox was intent on capitalizing on it.

Here, he gathered up all of the local Quaker leaders and engaged in a series of meetings that took place over the course of four days' time. George Fox's grand tour came to an end in the summer of 1673 when he finally boarded a ship and returned to Great Britain, confident that the many seeds he had planted in the New World would take root.

Chapter 2: William Penn Comes to the Quaker Faith

Did we believe a final reckoning and judgment; or did we think enough of what we do believe, we would allow more love in religion than we do; since religion itself is nothing else but love to God and man. Love is indeed heaven upon Earth; since heaven above would not be heaven without it. For where there is not love; there is fear. But perfect love casts out fear. Love is above all; and when it prevails in us all, we shall be lovely, and in love with God and one with another.

-William Penn

As powerful as the Quakers had become in Maryland, Pennsylvania would become the true bastion of the faith. Pennsylvania was founded by William Penn, who took charge of the region through a royal grant awarded to him in 1681. With this royal mandate, Penn would go on to create a government in Pennsylvania that would not only embrace the religious freedom that the Quakers craved but also many of the other essential American freedoms that the United States would someday hold dear.

Penn himself came to the Quaker faith as a young man. His first encounter with the Quakers occurred when he was just thirteen years old when his father Admiral Penn had a Quaker friend named

Thomas Loe come over to his home and preach to his family. This seems to have been a spur of the moment decision, but it would have lasting consequences for the admiral's son.

Like most British people at the time, Admiral Penn was a member of the Church of England. Yet he was still openminded enough to hear other people's points of view and beliefs. During this session, Admiral Penn's son, William Penn, first got a taste of Quakerism and came to admire the faith. His eyes were opened to the possibilities that day, and he would never forget the words that Mr. Loe had preached.

He learned of the inner light Quakers claimed inhabited all human beings, which allowed them to have a direct channel of communication with God. According to the tenets of Quakerism, we all have this divine light within us that we can tap into it at any time. This concept was mind-blowing for someone who grew up believing that there was a distinct separation between man and his creator.

Loe taught that this direct line of contact made preachers, churches, sacraments, and any other ritualized service completely unnecessary. There was no need for an intermediary of any kind. According to Loe, all one had to do was quiet themselves down and consult the inner light within. By doing this, they would be in direct communion with their very creator. William Penn was absolutely spellbound by what he had heard, and thus, the seeds of Quakerism were planted in the young boy.

The idea that one could have such a rock of stability within themselves was certainly appealing considering the tumultuous times in which they lived. England was in the throes of severe political instability. The nation had suffered a civil war, and from 1653 to 1658, it was being controlled by a former general turned dictator: Oliver Cromwell.

Officially known as the "Lord Protector," Cromwell had usurped power from the deposed King Charles II, with whom William Penn's father had been on good terms. Nevertheless, despite the loss of this royal benefactor, Admiral Penn found his footing under Cromwell, who made him "Rear Admiral of the Irish Seas," as well as "Vice Admiral in command of England's Third Fleet." By 1653, the older Penn was made "General at Sea," a role he carried with distinction.

Nevertheless, the thin ice underneath Admiral Penn's feet began to crack shortly after, and in just a few years' time, he was tossed into the horrid dungeon known as the Tower of London. The reason? He was believed to have somehow been in cahoots with the deposed King Charles II. Admiral Penn was only imprisoned for about five weeks, but the incident would leave a lasting mark on both him and his family.

It was after his release and his return to his homestead in Ireland, called "Macroom Castle," that the admiral invited Quaker minister Thomas Loe to say a word or two. Considering the circumstances, the Penn family was perhaps well dispositioned to hear the stirring message this Quaker conveyed. The idea that God's inner light rested in everyone and could not be taken away by tyrannical despots must have been appealing. And the younger Penn certainly never forgot the sermon delivered by Loe that day, as he held this precious moment dear to his heart.

Several years later, in 1667, after Cromwell had been removed and King Charles II restored to the throne, the now grown-up William Penn heard the same Quaker minister was back in town holding a meeting. William Penn's heart must have been stirred with fond memories of that day back at Macroom Castle, for he didn't hesitate to attend.

Penn apparently stood out from the outset due to his aristocratic dress. All the Quakers wore plain clothing, whereas Penn was decked out in the best finery of the day. Who was this wealthy looking young man who dared to attend a meeting of the Society of Friends? Quaker meetings at this time were illegal, and anyone in attendance was subject to arrest. It was a dangerous prospect for Penn just to attend.

William Penn had a lot going for him at the time. As the son of a British admiral, he was groomed for the finer things of British society. The idea that he would visit such a fringe group would have struck most of his peers as madness. He had a lot to lose being associated with the Quakers, yet William Penn still couldn't help but feel compelled to revisit the Quaker doctrine that had stirred his soul as a child.

William Penn was indeed taking a risk, and the precariousness of his situation was soon proven when the local authorities decided to break up the gathering. Someone must have tipped off the locals because this particular meeting was interrupted when one of the king's soldiers came barging right in.

It is interesting to note that only one man was initially tasked with shutting down the meeting. Since the Quakers were known to be nonviolent, this lone enforcer counted on the fact that the Quaker faithful would not resist his efforts. The Quakers who did indeed eschew violent action of any kind did not do anything to impede the intruder's advance.

Penn, who was not yet a Quaker, didn't hesitate, and he rushed to greet the interloper. This authority figure was no doubt shocked to see a finely dressed young man—someone who appeared to be of nobility no less—suddenly rush forward to greet him. William Penn seized hold of the man and appeared to be ready to do his worst, before some of the Quakers managed to convince Penn to let him go.

But if William Penn or his Quaker friends thought the government enforcer would simply shrug off the incident and forget about it, they were mistaken. The man took off only to return a short while later with more troops. This time, there was nothing Penn could do. He and all of the Quakers who were at the meeting were taken into custody and made to answer to a court magistrate.

After being released from jail, William was summoned by his father to explain what was going on. When Penn showed up with a Quaker friend in tow—one Josiah Coale, a man who was a known rabble-rouser among non-Quakers—Admiral Penn only became more agitated. Wishing to speak with his son alone, Admiral Penn took William to the side and began to question him as to what he was doing.

Even the manner of William Penn's speech offended his father, as William had since adopted the Quaker habit of referring to everyone as "thee" and "thou." Quakers did this in order to deny any acknowledgment of rank or status among people. The Quakers believed (and still do believe) that all were equal, as everyone had the same spark of divine light within them, and they refused to reference any sense of superior status.

In the Old English vernacular of the day, the terms "thee" and "thou" were used when speaking to commoners or the young, whereas the term "you" was used when addressing elders, especially those who had high-ranking social positions, as was the case with Admiral Penn. Taking umbrage to what he felt was a blatant show of disrespect, Admiral Penn chastised his son's speech, telling him that he "must use 'you' in speaking to older people or persons of high ranks."

His son was in his twenties at this point, but Admiral Penn must have felt that he was suddenly correcting a five-year-old. After all, everyone in English society knew better than to disrespect their elders like this. But William Penn's choice of words was not due to a lack of education or an intent to willfully disrespect anyone; he had simply been enlightened by the Quaker view that all should be equal under God, with no distinction showed whatsoever.

William Penn explained as much to his father. As his frustrated old man listened, William preached about how God was "no respecter of persons," and since God did not recognize status or rank, he and his Quaker brethren showed no such distinction either. Admiral Penn, however, was not too pleased by the sudden spiritual epiphany his son was having.

When Admiral Penn surmised that his son wanted to become a Quaker, he was immediately opposed to it. It's rather ironic that Admiral Penn was the one who had introduced his son to the Quaker faith in the first place yet was so displeased when the seed he had planted finally came to take root. Admiral Penn, who wished for his son to be a successful nobleman and not a Quaker fanatic, told his son of his displeasure in no uncertain terms and bid him to leave the family estate. William was essentially kicked out of the house.

Undaunted, Penn continued to pursue his beliefs. In fact, his father tossing him off the family estate only drove him further into the arms of the Quakers. From this point forward, William lived and breathed Quakerism. He not only went to Quaker meetings, but he also lived with Quakers. If necessary, he was willing to go to jail with them. During this period, William Penn even wrote religious tracts for the faith.

One of these, a tract entitled, *The Sandy Foundation Shaken*, landed him in some real hot water with the Church of England. The tract criticizes basic tenets of the Church of England's' doctrine, and when the Bishop of London got a hold of it in 1668, he was absolutely indignant and asked for William Penn to be arrested. For this simple little tract, which criticized the Church of England, William Penn was thrown into the Tower of London.

The Tower of London had served as a jail for all manner of dissenters. These people were cruelly tortured and, at times, executed. As such, it was certainly not a good place for William Penn to be in, by any stretch of the imagination. Nevertheless, when William Penn was given a chance to denounce Quakerism and be set free, he held firm, proclaiming, "My prison shall be my grave before I will budge a jot."

But very much in the tradition of George Fox who had come before him, William finally wrote an apologist treatise, in which he clarified his views and denied ever willfully hurting the Church of England, rejecting Christ, or disparaging the king. This was apparently enough for King Charles II, who was on good terms with William's father, and he had William Penn released from the Tower of London on July 28th, 1669.

The year 1669 was a pretty significant one for King Charles II, for he forged his infamous "CABAL" during this time. King Charles's cabal was a special council he created that consisted of his most trusted advisors. The name "cabal" actually comes from the first letter of each of the members' first names. The men on his cabal council were Clifford, Arlington, Buckingham, Ashley, and Lauderdale.

It was with this group of advisors that King Charles II would seek to further his policies. Due to the British government's tumultuous nature at the time, he needed this special council to help him push forward his aims. Yes, even though Charles II was king, he still had to strategize and finagle just like anyone else to get things done.

Charles II, who himself was secretly a Catholic, was constantly viewed with suspicion by his Protestant peers. Just about any move he made was held with equal suspicion. Even the simple act of setting William Penn free was met with harsh words and sniping criticism behind the king's back. Many undoubtedly felt the king was wasting his time with a religious reprobate who would never change his ways.

And sure enough, scarcely a month later, Penn ran afoul of the authorities once again. On August 14th, he was found preaching on the street in front of a closed meetinghouse to a large group of people. The sermon was quickly disrupted when the "sheriff and soldiers arrived" on the scene. William Penn was arrested by the sheriff and charged with "preaching seditiously and causing mayhem."

During this stint in jail, William's chief complaint was apparently over an interview the mayor made, in which the city leader made disparaging remarks about his father, Admiral Penn. From his prison cell, William wrote his father, explaining that while he "could bear harsh words about himself," he would not stand for verbal abuse being hurled at his dad. The mayor had apparently trudged up old criticisms, such as his father was a poor ship captain and that he "had starved his seamen," among other insults.

Such petty remarks were no doubt meant to rile up William Penn rather than actually injure the old admiral. And it seemed to work. Out of all the indignities William Penn suffered, nothing seemed to agitate him more than seeing his father being denigrated like this. Perhaps his knee-jerk reaction to defend his father's legacy inspired him to reach some sort of reconciliation with the admiral.

In his letter, Penn wrote his dear old dad the following: "Be not displeased or grieved. What if this be designed of the Lord for an exercise of our patience? I am very well and have no trouble upon my spirits, besides absence from thee."

Considering the fact that Admiral Penn had witnessed quite a transformation in his son, it was still hard for him to wrap his head around what was happening. Penn, a young man who previously seemed to have a promising future ahead of him, was suddenly being thrown in and out of jail and becoming associated with those considered to be on the margins of society. His son asked him to "exercise patience," and Admiral Penn probably was indeed having to pray for more than a little patience when it came to dealing with what he perceived to be his wayward son.

And it was probably with a heavy sigh that Admiral Penn read the last sentence of this letter. Because even though his son affirms his love for his father, he ends the missive with that ever so troubling pronoun of "thee." If it wasn't clear before, it must have seemed absolutely certain now to the old admiral that his son would never leave the Quaker faith.

Chapter 3: William Penn's Holy Experiment

We are inclined to call things by the wrong names. We call prosperity happiness, and adversity misery, even though adversity is the school of wisdom and often the way to eternal happiness.

–William Penn

William Penn languished in prison for two weeks before he was sent to trial on September 1ˢᵗ, 1670. He was tried on charges of holding an unlawful assembly and otherwise disturbing "the peace." Penn pleaded not guilty to all charges. As the trial convened, Penn and his fellow Quakers became ensnared by the prosecution in their refusal to remove their hats. In those days, it was common courtesy for someone to take off their hat when inside a courtroom, but for the Quakers, who refused to recognize any distinction of rank or authority other than God, this proved to be an impossible feat.

The prosecutors took note of this fact and used it as a means of attack every chance they could. Pretty soon, the Quaker defendants were being threatened with heavy court fines if they continued to insist upon wearing their hats. By the time Penn was called to the stand, he was defiant. He stated that he "would not recant" and would not even "validate" the charges against him since he believed they were unjust.

Penn then went on to state that he and his Quaker colleagues had the right to "preach, pray, or worship the Eternal, Holy, Just God" completely unhindered. He then advised that it was their "indispensable duty to meet incessantly upon so good an account; nor shall all the powers upon Earth be able to divert us from reverencing and adoring our God who made us."

The prosecution seemed to feel that this was simply grandstanding on Penn's part and insisted that he was not "on trial for worshipping God, but for breaking the law." Penn denied breaking any law and stated that the jury needed to have it explained to them just law he had supposedly broken so they would "know by what law it was that he was [being] prosecuted."

Not wanting to play this game, the court recorder simply snapped, "The Common Law!" He was unwilling to elaborate any further, stating that he would be unable to "run up so many years, and over so many adjudged cases which we call Common Law." Penn then shot back with the canny reply, "If it be common, it should not be so hard to produce."

Infuriated, the recorder resorted to name-calling, shouting, "You are a saucy fellow, speak to the indictment!" However, Penn was insistent, and he said, "You are many mouths and ears against me. I say again, unless you show me and the people the law you ground your indictment upon, I shall take it for granted and your proceedings are merely arbitrary."

The court recorder still continued to ignore Penn's argument and rejoined with "The question is whether you are guilty of this indictment." But William Penn continued to argue. "The question is not whether I am guilty of this indictment but whether this indictment be legal. Where there is no law there is no transgression." A heated back and forth followed before the recorder finally rebuked Penn, telling him, "Sir, you are a troublesome fellow, and it is not the honour of the Court to suffer you to go on."

Finally reaching his limit, the recorder eventually called for Penn to be confined to the back of the courtroom while the proceedings continued without him. Still, Penn would not be silent, and shouting from the "bail dock" where he was being held, he challenged, "Who are my judges?" Directing his remarks to the jury, he then shouted, "You of the Jury take notice that I have not been heard."

Fed up, it was at this point the court officials decided to have Penn and his associates taken out of the courtroom entirely and placed in a separate holding cell while the proceedings commenced without them. The jury was then asked to render a verdict, but when four of the jurors refused to find the Quakers guilty, the court began to threaten and use abusive language against them. Nevertheless, no matter how many times they were threatened, those four jurors would not buckle, they would not break, and they would not find Penn and his Quaker brethren guilty of any crime.

For this reason, the infuriated prosecution decided to hold Penn and his comrades for their failure to pay the fines leveled against them for refusing to take off their hats in court. William Penn knew his father would most likely pay this fee so that he could be released, but William wrote him a letter, specifically asking him not to do so.

William wrote his father, saying, "I intreat thee not to purchase my liberty...I would rather perish than release myself by so indirect a course as to satiate their revengeful, avaricious appetites. The advantage of such freedom would fall very short of the trouble of accepting it. Let not this wicked world disturb thy mind, and whatever shall come to pass, I hope in all conditions to prove thy obedient son."

Admiral Penn, of course, would not stand by and allow his son to rot in jail, so he indeed came to his son's rescue. The admiral not only bailed William out but also all of his Quaker associates as well. This would prove to be the last act of benevolence that the admiral would show toward his son since he was seriously ill and already close to death at the time, a fact the old admiral stoically acknowledged when he wrote his reply to William.

His father's letter read: "Son William, if you and your friends keep to your plain way of preaching, and keep to your plain way of living, you will make an end of the priests to the end of the world. Bury me by my mother. Live all in love." Time was indeed short for Admiral Penn, but his son was released just in time to be by his father's side when he finally passed on September 16th, 1670.

William would get in and out of trouble due to his Quaker beliefs quite frequently in the first few years following his father's passing. During this time, he also met and fell in love with a woman who strongly believed in the Quaker faith: Gulielma Maria Springett. She was the stepdaughter of a prominent Quaker by the name of Isaac Penington. As the son of the former mayor of London, Isaac Penington held great influence, and he used this to shape the early Quaker faith. William Penn and his new bride would likewise follow his lead, first in England and then in places much farther afield.

William Penn would first become involved in the New World when he was approached in 1675 by a couple of Quakers who had large property holdings in what was then known as "West Jersey." Penn, who was knowledgeable of the law by training, was tapped to forge a constitution for the region, which he called "Concession and Agreements." This document outlined the religious freedoms the Quakers desired and the kind of democracy they craved.

In many ways, this charter for West Jersey (later to become Pennsylvania) was a forerunner of what the actual United States Constitution would entail. "Concession and Agreements" contains general guidelines for the community, with an additional listing of allowed civil liberties, which are very much in line with what would eventually become the US Bill of Rights. William Penn, who lived one hundred years before the founding of the United States, is not usually considered a Founding Father, but there are those who would argue that he very well should be.

After creating this document, events unfolded rather rapidly, which put William Penn into a position of not just writing out legal charters for land but rather gaining land himself. Some of the original landholders began to sell off portions of their land, and Penn received some of them since he was one of the acting trustees. In 1680, the Duke of York (who would one day become King James II) gave even more holdings to Penn and some of his Quaker associates. On March 4th, 1681, none other than King Charles II himself granted William Penn some 46,000 square miles of colonial land in America.

It was King Charles II who decided to change the name of the colony to Pennsylvania. The appellation came from the Penn family name, with the notable addition of "sylvan," which is Latin for "forest land." According to some accounts, it was William Penn who initially came up with the idea to call the place "Sylvania," but it was King Charles II who added Penn in front of the term, rendering the name to be Pennsylvania.

Not surprisingly, William Penn, a modest Quaker, immediately rejected having his name attached to the colony. Upon hearing of it, he complained to King Charles II, telling him, "I feared lest it would be looked upon as a vanity in me and not as a respect in the King, as it truly was to my father whom he often mentions in praise." Attempting to pacify the Quaker's concerns, the king artfully deflected the perceived accolades, informing him, "We will keep it, my dear fellow, but not on your account, do not flatter yourself, we will keep the name to commemorate the Admiral, your noble father."

So, Penn had expressed reservations about having a colony named after him only for the king to basically tell him, "Oh! You thought I was naming the land after you? No way! It's being named after your dad!" Whether the king sincerely was naming the property after Admiral Penn or just wishing to present the matter in a way that would be more palatable to William Penn is anyone's guess. Perhaps it was a little bit of both. Admiral Penn was, after all, a well-respected man, and even William Penn would find it hard to refuse the colony being named in his honor. So, it was with this little change of perspective that William Penn agreed to allow Pennsylvania to be born.

Penn had called the land "Sylvania" due to the massive forests that blanketed the region. And in those rugged frontier days, Pennsylvania was indeed little more than a wooded forest. It was in this vast, untamed wilderness that Penn wished to conduct a "holy experiment," as he wished to plant and cultivate the full fruits of religious freedom.

Now that William had this land, he had to figure out how to govern it. In the charter for Pennsylvania, he was determined to create a bastion of liberty and tolerance. Unlike the surrounding colonies, in which someone could be summarily executed on the flimsiest of grounds (Mary Dyer was executed in Massachusetts simply for being a visiting Quaker), Penn made sure that the death penalty would only be enacted for those who had been convicted of murder or "high treason."

In April 1681, Penn sent his cousin, William Markham, to preside as the region's deputy governor, while he stayed behind to tie up loose ends in England. Markham washed up on the shores of Pennsylvania that summer, but he didn't come alone. He came armed with a rather long-winded epistle from William Penn, which set out in exact detail what he expected the future of Pennsylvania to be. To understand Penn's frame of mind better, here is his written directive in full:

> My friends: I wish you all happiness, here and hereafter. These are to let you know that it hath pleased God, in his providence, to cast you within my lot and care. It is a business that, though I never undertook before, yet God has given me an understanding of my duty, and an honest mind to do it uprightly. I hope you will not be troubled at your change and the King's choice, for you are now fixed at the mercy of no governor that comes to make his fortune great; you shall be governed by laws of your own making, and live a free and, if you will, a sober and industrious people. I shall not usurp the right of any, or oppress his person. God has furnished me with

a better resolution, and has given me his grace to keep it. In short, whatever sober and free men can desire for the security and improvement of their own happiness, I shall heartily comply with, and in five months I resolve, if it please God, to see you. In the meantime, pray submit to the commands of my deputy, so far as they are consistent with the law, and pay him those dues (that formerly you paid to the order of the Governor of New York) for my use and benefit, and so I beseech God to direct you in the way of righteousness, and therein prosper you and your children after you. I am your true friend. –William Penn

If the settlers in the region had worried over who would take control, this statement undoubtedly did much to allay their fears. In furtherance of this sentiment, Markham was given a prime directive by Penn to maintain healthy relations with those who already called Pennsylvania home, meaning the local Native American populations and the European settlers who were already maintaining a presence in the region.

Penn was especially mindful of not offending the Native Americans, instructing Markham "to be tender of offending the Indians." This approach was certainly fairly unique, setting Penn apart from his colonial contemporaries. Pennsylvania's constitution was also quite different from others, as it allowed many of the liberties that the future US Constitution would have, such as freedom of the press, trial by jury, and freedom of religion. Of course, the latter was crucial for the Quakers, as they had been terribly persecuted for their religion for many years. So, it is perhaps no surprise that Penn purposefully instituted a governance framework that would be friendly to the Quakers. Pennsylvania, which was noted in particular for its tolerance of Quakerism, would also become known as a haven for freedom of religion in general, and it would become fertile ground for a wide variety of religious expressions in the years to come.

Although he initially governed from afar, William Penn finally arrived in Pennsylvania on October 27th, 1682. Almost as soon as he arrived, he made it his priority to enter into peace talks and negotiations with the local Native American populations. The Native Americans were naturally suspicious of the newcomers and with good reason, considering that so many other European immigrants had been deceptive in their aims.

However, Penn wanted to make his good intentions clear, and he entered into the so-called "Great Treaty" with Native American leaders, in which he expressly stated that "no land could be taken away from them." Not only that, but he also made it a point to actually become friends with the local Native Americans who lived in the area. Penn would come and visit their homes, eat with them, speak with them in their own tongue, and even attend Native American festivities in an effort to show that he meant no harm.

King Charles II cautioned Penn, telling him that he needed to allow for an "armed force to protect the Quakers from the Indians." William Penn steadfastly refused. Penn resolutely told the king, "I want none of your majesty's soldiers." The king is then said to have asked, "But how will you get your lands without soldiers?"

This statement is indicative of what was really going on in Pennsylvania. Although the British had claimed the territory, and the king had given it over to Penn as if he was the owner of the land, both the king and William Penn knew that others already laid claim to it. It was for this reason that King Charles II suggested armed troops were needed to solidify the British grip on the territory and allow for further expansion as desired.

But the fact that the Native Americans had been there first was certainly not lost on Penn. And his response demonstrates how he viewed the whole situation. Without blinking, Penn answered, "I mean to buy their lands of them." Buying lands from Native Americans? This was certainly not what King Charles II was expecting to hear. And he practically shouted in response, "Why man—you have bought them of me already!"

Penn did not dispute the British concept that the Pennsylvanian wilderness had been titled, deeded, and handed over from the monarchy, but he didn't discount the Native Americans either. Penn thus replied, "Yes; I know I have, and at a dear rate too. I did this to gain thy good will, not that I thought thou hadst any right to their lands—I will buy the rights of the proper owners, even of the Indians themselves: by doing this, I shall imitate God in his justice and mercy, and hope thereby, to insure his blessing on my colony, if I should ever live to plant on in North America."

Penn demonstrated the perfect example of both Quaker humility and the Quaker sense of fairness and justice. If settling Pennsylvania had been wrong, William Penn was more than willing to make it right. And his efforts produced some rather immediate results because shortly after Markham explained his aims to the local Native American leaders, they declared that they would "live in peace" with the Quakers "as long as the sun and the moon shall endure."

The colonization of Pennsylvania ran its course at a fairly steady rate. It is said that between 1681 and 1682, some 23 different ships, carrying around 2,000 passengers altogether, arrived from England. On the ground, Markham had done well to fulfill William Penn's wishes in peacefully purchasing property from the Lenape. He made sure the purchases he made were contiguous, and with them, he slowly extended the range of the Pennsylvania Colony both north and south alongside the natural boundary of the Delaware River.

As soon as William Penn arrived on the scene, he began to handle the land purchases himself, and he negotiated several acquisitions. In the summer of 1683 alone, he managed to secure three huge tracts of land from various representatives of local tribes. These acquisitions were then followed by even more valuable territory nestled in the Brandywine River, which was acquired on November 19th, 1683. William Penn attempted to be as cordial as possible in his relations with the tribal groups and even went so far as to learn the language of the Lenape (also known as Delaware).

In the ensuing years, events made life harder for the British Quakers. British Parliament had been actively contesting the authority of King Charles II. They also decried the king's closeness with non-mainstream religious groups like the Quakers. This resulted in a backlash from the king, which led to tightening constraints on groups such as the Quakers. This overreach only ended when King Charles II abruptly died from a massive stroke a few months later. After his death, Charles's brother, James II (the former Duke of York), was crowned king in February of 1685. Although King James II was a staunch Catholic, he would become one of the greatest benefactors the Quaker faith had ever known.

Chapter 4: William Penn, Pennsylvania, and Its Quaker Legacy

I expect to pass through life but once. If therefore, there be any kindness I can show, or any good thing I can do to any fellow being, let me do it now, and not defer or neglect it, as I shall not pass this way again.

–William Penn

King James II was inaugurated as Britain's new monarch on February 6th, 1685. As it turns out, King James II would be the last Catholic king of England, yet despite his preference for Catholicism, he would be rather friendly to the Quakers. In fact, he had been a good friend of Admiral Penn's, and by extension, he was on good terms with his son as well. Although James was a Catholic, it was due to the words of his good friend William Penn that he came to understand and respect the Quaker faith, despite its differences from mainstream Christianity.

Penn was the one who convinced King James II that the values of the Quakers would not upset the social order but actually benefit it. James, though by no means thinking of converting to the faith himself, soon came to believe that the British government had nothing to fear from the Quakers. George Fox may have begun this trend when he penned his famous Peace Testimony, which explained the peaceful nature of the Quaker's intentions. But as far as King James II was concerned, it was William Penn who made these words a reality.

It was with this new understanding that King James II, who enacted sweeping religious reforms in the spring of 1686, began the process of pardoning those who had been thrown into jail over their religious beliefs. During this general amnesty, it is estimated that over 13,000 Quakers were given their freedom. But despite all of this goodwill toward other religions, the English elite feared having a Catholic monarch on the throne, and it wasn't long before courtiers began to grumble against him.

Due to the resistance Catholic King James II faced due to his faith, he could, in some sense, relate to the difficulties of the Quakers. This empathy added yet another layer to the mutual understanding between the king and William Penn. This understanding was evidenced by King James II's "Declaration of Indulgence," which went into effect on April 4th, 1687.

This declaration that did away with the enforcement of "penal laws," which had previously demanded adherence to the Church of England's orthodoxy. It also finally gave British subjects the official right to pursue their own religious inclinations, even if it went against the mainstream practices of the Anglican Church.

By helping religious minorities such as his Quaker friends, King James II was actually helping himself, for he saw greater religious tolerance in general as a means of making Catholicism more palatable in Britain. Penn was very close to the king around the time of this declaration, and some have suggested that Penn was the principal "instigator" in bringing it about.

Of course, the closeness between these two men would not go unnoticed, and it wasn't long before the king's enemies became William Penn's enemies.

Some of the other Protestant denominations, which despised the fact their reigning monarch was Catholic, began to deny Penn's Quakerism and made William Penn out to be a Catholic himself. Some even went so far as to call him "William, the Papist," indicating that Penn was under the sway of the Roman pope. Of course, this was not only ridiculous but absolutely false.

In fact, most people who lived in England at the time were probably aware of Penn's staunch Quakerism, yet this lie was propagated all the same. Back then, as is still the case today, falsehoods were sometimes actively promoted to bring down someone who a certain group did not like. And William Penn himself was unfortunate enough to fall into the crosshairs of such malicious liars.

These detractors actively sought a way to take Penn's benefactor, King James II, off the throne. Their opportunity came in the form of William of Orange, who was a Protestant from the Netherlands. British Parliament actually sent out a request for William of Orange to come and seize the kingship for himself. He accepted the offer, showing up with about 14,000 soldiers. King James II did not like his odds and fled to France.

This turn of events caused a lot of trouble for William Penn, who had made his way back to England by this time. Since he was on such good terms with King James II, he was suddenly viewed as being on the wrong side of history. Any friend of the deposed King James II was perceived as an enemy of the state, and this resulted in William Penn's arrest on December 10th, 1688, just as William of Orange was securing power for himself.

Made to answer for his past association with the now-deposed James II, William Penn stood strong and spoke his mind. Instead of groveling for mercy, he clearly stated his case. He told those who would listen that he "loved his country" and would never do anything to betray it. Penn denied the charges that he had been in league with the Catholic Church, and he also proclaimed his solidarity with the Protestants. Even though the Quakers were considered a fringe group, they were indeed counted as one of the many products of the Protestant Reformation.

However, Penn refused to renounce James II, not because he believed that all of his actions had been right, but because he simply viewed him as a trustworthy friend. Penn told his accusers that if he was loyal to the king, it was out of gratitude for how good he had been to him and his family. This only increased some of the calls for Penn's immediate execution, but luckily enough, Penn's honest, forthright answers won over the only person that really mattered—William of Orange.

The new king was not a fan of groveling, and so, he was impressed with Penn's bold stand. William of Orange, now King William III, had Penn released, and the charges against him were dropped. And to the horror of Penn's enemies, he ended up in the good graces of yet another British monarch. It was partially due to Penn's influence that William III presided over a Parliament that managed to pass the Act of Toleration, which ensured a relative degree of religious freedom in Britain.

In the meantime, Penn was routinely harassed by his political enemies, who were constantly looking for some reason to have William Penn hauled off to jail. This constant scrutiny led to Penn's arrest once again in 1690 when he was brought in on charges of having carried out correspondence with the dethroned James II. Once again, the charges didn't stick, and after a short time, Penn was released.

George Fox, the founder of Quakerism, passed away in 1691. Penn attended the funeral, where he gave a rousing speech. Immediately after the funeral service, he was alerted about plans for his arrest on charges of treason. This forced Penn to lay low for a while. However, Penn's low point was still to come, and it arrived in the spring of 1692. This was the year that William Penn lost control of Pennsylvania. King William III appointed a royal governor to preside over Pennsylvania instead.

The everyday persecution of Quakers had intensified greatly in the meantime, with random acts of violence and vandalism becoming commonplace. Unlike during the benevolent tolerance of King James II, the Quakers suddenly seemed to have no quarter. Seeming to voice the abrasive, intolerant sentiment of the times, a priest from Glasgow even went so far as to call Quakers, "Heretics, blasphemers, possessed with the devil and as dangerous to converse with as those that have the plague."

Considering that England had recently been struck with a terrible case of bubonic plague, for a preacher to label all Quakers as bad as the virulent strain of pestilence that was killing people left and right is pretty inflammatory, to say the least. And as might be expected, this kind of language only incensed those who opposed the Quakers. During this period, there were actually cases of mobs spontaneously gathering to "throw stones" at Quakers.

Despite this fierce opposition, the Quakers, who lived and breathed the New Testament, no doubt felt that this only showed they were living out the ideals of Christ. They cherished the words of the Good Book and saw direct parallels between the persecution of the saints of the Bible and the persecution they themselves faced. Biblical figures, such as Stephen, were stoned to death, Apostle Paul was stoned to death, and even Jesus himself was nearly stoned at one point. It is no wonder the Quakers thought they were in good company.

In fact, the Quakers were following a familiar script that has played out ever since the writing of the New Testament in the 1st century CE. Until religious tolerance was the norm in the Western world, every time a new religious mode of Christian thought popped up, the orthodoxy rose in opposition to stamp it out. This began with the first Christians themselves, and it continued with every new movement that emerged throughout the years.

George Fox, Martin Luther, and other early Christian thinkers, such as St. Thomas Aquinas and St. Augustine, were all inspired by the radical nature of the New Testament (after all, there is nothing quite as radical than a book that asks one to love their enemies), and they had visions of a better way to approach a personal relationship with God. They also had their own orthodox detractors who quickly rose up against their vision, crying out that those who dared to try a new approach to mainstream religion were "blasphemers."

The Quakers were indeed a part of this same religious cycle that had been repeating since Christianity's inception. They had become the new martyrs of the age, willing to die for their faith just like the heroes they had read about in the scriptures. But fortunately for the Quakers (or unfortunately, if some among them truly did have their hearts set on being martyrs), the political winds of Britain would shift once again, and the persecution would wane.

And as for William Penn himself? In 1693, some of William Penn's connections in the king's court managed to convince him to reinstate Penn's status. Penn was then given a "new charter" for Pennsylvania and was sent to be the governor of those Pennsylvanian woodlands once again. But there were a few strings attached to this reinstatement. For one thing, Penn was required to supply troops for Pennsylvania.

The king feared an imminent French invasion. King William III claimed he had reason to believe that French King Louis XIV, who just happened to be shielding his predecessor, James II, had designs on New York and Pennsylvania. Of course, this was quite a conundrum for a Quaker like William Penn, who abhorred violence. Whatever troops he gathered, they would have to be non-Quakers.

Before William Penn could sail to Pennsylvania, his life was disrupted by the death of his wife, Gulielma Maria Springett, on February 23rd, 1694. While he tried to handle his remaining affairs in England, he once again made William Markham governor in his absence. It wouldn't be until five years later that Penn would have his affairs well enough in order to set sail for Pennsylvania. Within that time, Penn had actually met and married another woman by the name of Hannah Callowhill, whom he wed in 1696.

It was with Hannah that he would return to stake his claim in Pennsylvania in the fall of 1699. By that time, William Penn was just about bankrupt after years of having to foot the various bills of Pennsylvania through his own pockets. The situation was so bleak that he considered selling his holdings back to the king. But before he did any such thing, Penn wanted to make sure that the state he left behind had remained strong.

The Quaker haven of Pennsylvania would become known for its fair and just treatment of the Native American tribes who lived nearby. This created much goodwill in the region, and it was this lasting legacy that granted Pennsylvania relative peace over the next several decades while other states faced routine skirmishes with nearby tribes. In fact, William Penn was so revered by the local Native Americans that they actually used him as a peace broker when fighting broke out between two different tribal groups.

William was definitely rare for the times he lived in, and his public policies proved it. In the spring of 1701, Penn held a meeting with the governor of Virginia and the governor of New York to brainstorm ways they could strengthen the ties between the states. Even though states like Pennsylvania, New York, and Virginia were basically separate entities, each with their own separate charters and beholden to the king, Penn argued for creating more unity and uniformity among them. He believed the colonies needed universal court practices, currency, and even a police force that could operate from colony to colony. Of course, this was what would happen one hundred some years later after the colonies gained independence, but when Penn championed these ideas back in 1701, his colleagues mostly just humored him. No one took it too seriously at the time.

Shortly after this conference, Penn found cause for alarm when he received word that the king of England planned to turn the colonies into "royal provinces." This would mean the colonies would be under the king's direct control, and the king would be able to arbitrarily appoint his own royal governors. Penn wasn't going to stand for that, so he left his Quaker brethren behind to head back to England once again. Before he left, he made sure the legislative body made an updated Pennsylvanian constitution that further enshrined the Quaker principles of peace, fair dealing, and benevolence.

Once this was settled, Penn set sail for England. William Penn showed up on the last day of the year—December 31st, 1701. When he arrived, he received word that the king had actually passed away during his voyage. This made James II's daughter, Queen Anne, the new reigning monarch.

William Penn and some of his Quaker entourage made their way to the queen's court to check the pulse of where the Quakers currently stood with the regime. The meeting apparently went well, and Queen Anne duly informed Penn, "You and your friends may be assured of my protection."

But even with Queen Anne's support, Penn's situation was rather grim. He learned that his old "agent," Philip Ford, had passed away. As it turned out, Ford had mishandled Penn's finances, made bad investments, and created a lot of debt. Ford's family then demanded Penn pay the leftover debt. Unable to pay it, Penn was actually sent to a debtors' prison in 1708. This was indeed a time in which people with outstanding debts could be sent to jail, and Penn would languish in a jail cell for the next several months.

Penn, of course, wasn't a stranger to confinement, but the fact that he was imprisoned over debt rather than religious persecution must have been quite a matter of embarrassment. It's one thing to go to jail fighting for what one believes in; it's another matter entirely to do time for failing to pay your bills. However, Penn was vindicated by his old Quaker friends, who managed to go through the financial records of the late Ford and found evidence of just how much Ford had swindled Penn out of money.

Taking this into consideration, the legal counsel strongly urged Ford's surviving family members to scale back on their demands. Finally, they accepted a settlement of 7,600 pounds. The same friends that uncovered Ford's corruption raised the money to pay off this settlement, and William Penn was freed.

Penn would live out the rest of his life in England. After suffering a stroke in 1712, his health would deteriorate, and he would finally die, some say "penniless," in 1718, at the age of seventy-four. But what he didn't have in money, he more than made up for in faith and the great legacy he left behind.

Chapter 5: The State of Quakerism after William Penn

Be patterns, be examples in all countries, places, islands, nations wherever you come; that your carriage and life may preach among all sorts of people, and to them; then you will come to walk cheerfully over the world, answering that of God in everyone; whereby in them you may be a blessing, and make the witness of God in them to bless you.

–George Fox

William Penn would pass away in 1718, but the example that William Penn had set for religious toleration would be continued by his further successors, who kept a steady social compact over the next few decades. It was his sons, Richard and Thomas Penn, as well as his grandson, John Penn, who would inherit the stewardship of Pennsylvania from William.

Immediately after William Penn's death, his wife Hannah took over the administration of Pennsylvania—a role she would serve until her own passing in 1726. After Hannah's death, Thomas, who was Hannah and William's son, would run the colony for nearly forty years in an arrangement that had him named as the "managing proprietor." Thomas proved to have the same knack for management that his father had, but his religious views differed. In fact, Thomas would opt to leave the Quaker church altogether and join up with the Church of England instead.

This would have been completely abhorrent to his father since William had struggled so hard to be free from the Church of England's grip for most of his life. But where his father attempted to stand his own ground and set himself apart from the status quo, Thomas seemed more inclined to go with the flow. He was described as "prosperous, accomplished, sensible," and a "cool-headed gentleman."

Thomas was not the firebrand that his father was, as he would much rather polish his social skills and fit into conventional norms than go against the grain as his dad had. Thomas was also much more pragmatic and careful with his finances, whereas his father William Penn didn't hesitate to spend large amounts of his own money, often to his own detriment.

To his credit, Thomas attempted to keep much of his father's social policies intact in the colony. He did his best to maintain the liberties set down in Pennsylvania's charter while struggling to make sure the British monarch in power was happy with the results. This was certainly not an easy balancing act.

It also must not have been easy to make sure that the settlers and Native Americans didn't rub each other the wrong way. Thomas, who upheld his father's pledge for fair dealings with the Native American tribes, tried his best to make sure that land deals were appropriate and that tensions never boiled out of control. Initially, the policies of William Penn were continued, but dishonesty and malfeasance, especially as it pertained to the local Native Americans who had dealings in the region, eventually began to seep in.

This can be seen in the infamous "Walking Purchase of 1737." In this dreadful episode, the trickery employed by greedy settlers who wanted Native American land was at its worst. The purchase revolved around a group of local Delaware, who measured their land by the "walking distance" of one day. They apparently agreed to sell some of their property along the Delaware River based on these measurements, and this was where settlers saw an opportunity for deception.

They used their own surveyors to walk the distance and apparently had their "fastest walkers" halfway run up the river so that the distance traveled would equal more land than the Delaware intended to sell. When the incredulous Delaware balked at the measurements, the settlers, instead of admitting their trickery, called in a militia from New York, who forcibly made the Delaware leave their property. The Delaware tribe would not forget this treachery and would become a bitter nemesis to the Pennsylvanian settlers after that.

By the 1750s, the pacifism that had been so carefully fostered by the Quakers began to give way to naked aggression. Outright conflict emerged in 1755, most notably with the Penn's Creek massacre, in which settlers were slaughtered by the Lenape (also known as the Delaware) tribe. This led many nonviolent Quakers in the legislature to openly renounce their positions. And without the Quaker influence, Pennsylvania fell into open warfare.

However, even as Quakers left positions of power, they proved themselves to be powerful activists, standing up for Native Americans' rights and being among the first to call for the abolition of slavery. One of the most powerful advocates for the abolition of slavery was a man named John Woolman. Woolman was born in 1720 and developed a passion for justice and equality from a young age.

He was in his early twenties when he experienced something that would change his life. Woolman was working for a man who was selling a slave, and he was asked to personally arrange the transaction. It was his job as a clerk to compile any bill of lading his employer requested, but Woolman immediately knew in his heart that this particular sale was horribly wrong. And not only did he think it—he acted upon it. Woolman stood up to his boss, resolutely informing him that slavery was wrong and that he would not play any part of such an evil transaction.

From that day forward, he became a staunch advocate for abolition. He also became a dedicated Quaker minister, who ceaselessly preached about the "truth and light" within everyone. This is still a major Quaker theme today, one that had been developed by the Quaker founder George Fox.

Woolman was a sensitive man who truly cared about others. Even animals were not exempt from his compassion, as was indicated when he decided to shun the use of horses for transportation since he felt the animals were often treated cruelly. Yes, long before animal cruelty was even really a concept, this sympathetic Quaker became a passionate advocate for animal rights.

Woolman traveled far and wide, spreading his views on Quakerism. He also spread his views on the evils of slavery. He continued to denounce slavery in both his words and his actions. It's said that whenever he visited someone's home that had slaves in the household, he always made sure to pay the slaves for whatever services they rendered, and he made sure to confront the slave owners about the practice.

And for Woolman, these things usually went hand in hand. For example, if someone in bondage served John Woolman dinner, he would hand them money for their work. And if the slave owner questioned him about it, which they often did, this opened the door for Woolman to condemn the practice to the slave owner's face. With the help of Woolman's tireless crusade against slavery, Quaker minds began to shift and become much more resolute on denouncing the practice.

By 1750, they were more or less convinced of the evils of slavery and began proactive measures to stem the tide of the practice. The Quakers began to see slavery as not only detrimental to those who were in bondage but also to those who held them there. First and foremost, they saw enforced servitude as not only a denial of the rights of the enslaved but also a covering up of their "inward light." Again, the Quakers believe that we each have an inward manifestation of God that needs to be allowed to shine bright. Just think of the kid's song, "This little light of mine—I'm gonna let it shine!" The Quakers believe that God's light dwells within all of us and should not be hindered. Therefore, they believed it a terrible travesty that the darkness of slavery covered up the inward light of the enslaved.

The Quakers also saw the practice as dimming the inward light of the slave owners as well. How could God's light shine through a person when they were engaged in such a horrid enterprise as slavery? The Quakers believed that the slave owner's light was greatly diminished by exploiting the labor of others. That's not to say the Quakers themselves never had slaves, as some among them most certainly did. From the Caribbean island of Barbados to the Southern United States, there were Quakers who ran plantations. And besides the Quakers who actively took part in slavery, there were also those who didn't own slaves yet indirectly benefited from the practice. Cotton merchants, for example, would have been less likely to find fault in slavery since their income partially depended upon it.

As it pertains to universally condemning the practice, real progress was made in 1758 when the Quakers launched an official edict stating that any Quakers who had slaves needed to "to be labored with." In other words, they needed a stern dressing-down. This meant that even though slave-owning Quakers would not be kicked out of the Quaker faith outright, they would not be allowed to attend meetings and would be excluded from many other aspects of church life. Some might have seen this as the Quakers shunning others of the same faith, while others might have viewed it as common decency that would help pave the way for a better, more tolerant future. Either way, slave-owning Quakers were ostracized for their participation in slavery.

The next major milestone in the Quakers' quest to rid slavery from their ranks occurred in 1770 at the "New England Yearly Meeting," when it was determined that any Quakers who had slaves had to take steps toward their emancipation. This then culminated into a Quaker-wide declaration being made in 1784, which demanded that all Quakers take immediate measures to free their slaves. If they did not, they would lose their membership in the church.

So, less than a decade after the American Revolution, the Quakers were staunchly opposed to slavery. And their efforts bore immediate fruit, as they were able to not only convince some slave owners to free their slaves but also aided runaway slaves in gaining freedom. These efforts would culminate in the Quakers participating in the Underground Railroad.

Up until the abolition of slavery, the Underground Railroad served as an active conduit for the transportation of runaway slaves to the North. However, this "railroad" did not depend on railroad tracks or train cars. It depended on dedicated men and women who agreed to transform their homes into secret "stations," at which runaways could stop and rest while they were on their trek to freedom.

The Quakers' role in this elaborate system of sheltering and stewarding runaway slaves to the North cannot be understated. The Underground Railroad gave African American men, women, and children, who lived in bondage in the Southern states, hope that they could find deliverance if they just made their way to the North. Not only that, but the continued stream of runaways helped to eat away at the entire slave system of the South. The Southern slave system could have no sense of security as long as groups like the Quakers actively aided and abetted runaways.

It was out of desperation to stop this migration to the North that Southerners pushed for the so-called Fugitive Slave Laws of 1850, demanding that they had the right to bring runaways who made their way north back to the South. It was this draconian measure that would increase tensions between the abolitionists of the North and the slaveholders of the South until an all-out civil war finally erupted to settle the score once and for all.

Along with these general contributions to the eventual abolition of slavery, it is also said that the Quakers were integral in ensuring slavery did not exist any farther north than Maryland. The Quakers had quite literally drawn a line in the sand when it came to slavery, and they rose up in deliberate action to make sure the terrible practice of bondage would not be allowed to propagate itself any more than it already was.

The Quakers having such a strong voice in these matters speaks volumes to their influence. This once little-known sect from England now made a substantial impact in the United States. Although the years after Penn's death were filled with plenty of ups and downs, Quakerism was still a strong force to be reckoned with, both in North America and beyond.

Chapter 6: Quaker Life during the American Revolution

All that dwell in the light, their habitation is in God, and they know a hiding place in the day of storm; and those who dwell in the light, are built upon the rock, and cannot be moved, for who are moved or shaken, goes from the light, and so goes from their strength, and from the power of God, and loses the peace and the enjoyment of the presence of God.

–Edward Burrough

The American Revolution was a time of radical reorganization of thought as it pertained to society and how people should be governed. Many Protestants were supportive of these efforts from the beginning, as they were under the idea that putting distance between their own ideologies and the dictates of the Church of England would most likely be in their best interest.

On the other hand, the Quakers faced their most difficult period in America during the American Revolution, which lasted from 1776 to 1783. As pacifists, the Quakers were against war in all forms, and so, they were quite naturally against an armed uprising against the British Crown. This refusal to side with the American freedom fighters put the Quakers under immediate suspicion.

They were sometimes cast as Loyalists, even though, at least for the Quakers, it was much more complicated than that. Most of them simply eschewed violence and bloodshed of any kind. The idea of an armed revolt was out of the question for most of them. Although the Quakers were against the war, some did side with the American revolutionaries, at least on an ideological level. They recognized the freedom the Founding Fathers promised would be much greater than anything the Crown had ever offered them.

Still, most Quakers were shunned and viewed as "security risks." And due to their peaceful and friendly disposition, they sometimes were. For instance, in the winter of 1777/78, some Quakers rendered aid to the British forces in Philadelphia. The Quakers undoubtedly felt they were doing their Christian duty to aid the struggling British, but this led to at least one of these collaborators being executed by the American revolutionaries.

In some instances, Quakers were held indefinitely without any clear charges other than vague accusations of "treason." This happened to a Quaker man by the name of Henry Drinker. He was arrested and detained in the fall of 1777. Drinker was held behind bars and told to swear allegiance to the American government. When he refused, he was then shuttled off in a wagon and dumped in Virginia, where he was an unwanted exile as punishment.

This treatment of the Quakers seemed to harken back to the puritanical 1650s when colonial authorities routinely banished Quakers from their communities. Despite its best intentions for a more equitable society, the American Revolution was most certainly a time of hardship and uncertainty for the Society of Friends. Whether they admitted it or not, many of the Quakers remained essentially loyal to Britain and simply did not see revolt and revolution as a good course of action.

Of course, this sentiment would lead to much friction with their fellow Americans, but it was a decidedly complicated situation. For one thing, the Quakers in America still had strong ties to the Quakers in England, and their British counterparts always advised their colonial brethren not to stir up trouble, lest they jeopardize these fraternal ties.

There was also a little bit of petty grudge-holding involved in the decision among some Quakers to stay neutral. Many of the American Quakers were not always treated the best by the local American Revolution leaders, which led to a natural wariness of being involved in any uprising engineered by those who had been less than kind to them.

Despite all of the reasons not to encourage fighting, a few Quakers were involved with the American Revolution. One of them, a man named Stephen Hopkins, even signed his name on the Declaration of Independence. To be fair, Hopkins was a former Quaker since he had actually been kicked out due to his refusal to emancipate his slaves.

There were also the rare Quakers who ignored the Quaker tenets of nonviolence and suited up with the Continental Army. One such Quaker was a young man by the name of Charles Darragh. Darragh was from a notable Quaker family in Pennsylvania; his father, William, was a teacher, and his mother, Lydia, was a midwife. Despite any misgivings these stalwart Quakers may have had, their son joined the Continental Army to serve under the 2nd Pennsylvania Regiment.

Although Charles was the one to enlist, it was actually his mother who would prove to be the most invaluable. When the British began to occupy the region, Lydia, who kept a line of communication open with her son, began to provide him with invaluable intelligence as to the movement of British troops.

In the fall of 1777, the Brits took over all of Philadelphia, and British General William Howe set up shop right inside Lydia Darragh's home. The British were indeed an occupying force, and if they wanted to make use of someone else's living quarters, there wasn't much the residents could do about it. The British most likely felt they had nothing to fear from the Quakers since they were known to be avowed pacifists.

But little did General Howe know that one of the Quakers he had barged in on—Lydia—was quite adept at gathering information! Soon, the staff meetings General Howe regularly hosted in Lydia's abode were subject to a major leak of vital intel, which was siphoned off by Lydia herself and fed directly into the ears of the men fighting in the American Revolution.

The British seemed to be blithely unaware of this fact, and General Howe continued to hold planning sessions in her home. At one point, in December of 1777, he even went so far as to tip Lydia off that a "major meeting" was about to take place, advising her to go to sleep a little early that night, lest she be disturbed. It seems General Howe wasn't very worried about being spied upon; rather, he was just trying to be polite.

Well, Lydia was not about to sleep through all of this chatter from the enemy and instead stayed up. Unbeknownst to the general, she sat right by the closed door so she could listen to every single word. From this session, Lydia learned the British were planning a sneak attack on the Continental Army arrayed outside of the city, which was led by General George Washington.

Lydia certainly knew she had discovered something of major import, and she was determined to let the revolutionary soldiers among know about it. As soon as she was sure the meeting was about to come to a close, Lydia carefully made her way back to bed. The next day, Lydia sought and was given permission to leave British-occupied territory so she could purchase some groceries. But she was determined to do more than shopping that day. She ended up dropping off her "empty bag" she used to shop with at a local mill and made a bee-line for the camp of General George Washington instead. Lydia was then able to impart what she had learned to the revolutionaries.

Thanks to Lydia's intel, when the British tried to launch their surprise attack on Washington's troops, they were prepared. Instead of being surprised, the Americans were able to launch a ferocious counterattack of their own and send the British running for the hills. And all of this was thanks to one meek and mild Quaker woman who decided to intervene. The British actually questioned Lydia later on when they discovered their operation had been compromised, but in the end, they never believed her to be a spy. Nevertheless, it was due to Lydia's heroics that many American lives were saved that day.

Another Quaker woman who found herself in a very similar position during the war was a North Carolinian by the name of Martha Bell. Martha and her husband owned a gristmill that specialized in making flour. As the war heated up between the Americans and the British, her gristmill was overrun by British troops, which began to regularly seize ground corn flour and other supplies from the mill.

Although Martha and her husband supported the revolutionary cause, they didn't hesitate to help the enemy British troops occupying their property. For a Quaker, all life is precious, even those with whom you ideologically may disagree. Martha frequently tended the wounds of the British troops, while her husband helped grind corn into flour at the mill.

During this time, the Bells seemed to gain the favor of the occupying general, who promised them that "no harm would come to their property." Martha would later use this assurance to her advantage when she went to visit the British encampment later on. By this point, the Brits had moved on from the mill, but Martha visited the British camp anyway, pretending to be concerned over some damage done to her property.

However, this was just a ruse. Martha made up this scheme so she could take note of enemy positions, troop numbers, and armaments—all vital intelligence information she hoped to gather for the revolutionaries. She was then able to take all of this valuable data back to the revolutionary troops, giving them astoundingly accurate information about the capabilities of this British regiment and where they were most likely to head next.

All of this Quaker cloak and dagger activity was certainly helpful for the cause of the American Revolution. But most of these efforts were virtually unknown to the rest of the population. Besides these unsung Quaker heroes, the most notable Quakers who decided to throw in their lot with the revolutionary cause were the so-called "Free Quakers" of Philadelphia, Pennsylvania. They were founded in 1781. The most well-known member was a woman by the name of Betsy Ross, who would go on to allegedly design the first American flag.

But Quakers like Betsy were the rare few, and the rest of the Quakers mostly just tried to keep their heads down. Some were even forced to lay low. Quakers wanted to avoid fates of being shunted about, as was the case with many Philadelphian Quakers. They were relocated to Virginia's backwoods since they were deemed untrustworthy and potential "security risks."

The Quakers also naturally got into trouble when revolutionary authorities began to request "oaths of loyalty" from citizens. The Quakers had long sworn off any kind of oathtaking, so they, of course, fell short whenever they were called upon to pledge their allegiance to the American war effort. In some instances, Quakers were fined for failing to participate with local militias, which many other local citizens were doing. Such things became increasingly hard to avoid, as many of the key battles fought in the Revolutionary War occurred in places heavily populated by Quakers.

And for those Quakers who did join militias and take up arms for the cause of the American Revolution, they faced immediate repercussions from their local Quaker meeting house. Since Quakers were supposed to uphold nonviolence, many of these Patriot Quakers were excommunicated for their actions. Those who were shunned by their local Quaker leaders often found an accepting place in the Society of Free Quakers, which had been formed in Philadelphia.

Here, Quakers who actively supported the war effort could support one another.

It was indeed a difficult and confusing time to be a Quaker. Nevertheless, by the time the war came to its conclusion, most of the Quakers were able to reconcile with both the newly established United States of America and with each other. Quakers also had to reconcile the fact that much of the power they had held over state legislatures and other colonial power structures had mostly been demolished.

For those that longed for the glory days of William Penn, this was a dispiriting situation. But for the hardcore orthodox Quakers who wanted to get back to their roots and be free of the burden of politics, this severance of political ties came as a relief. They believed it was a means of moving the Quakers "away from the world and its enticements."

Even as their temporal power began to recede, the spiritual power of the Quakers entered into a great awakening all of its own. Soon, there was a renewed interest in what it meant to be a Quaker and how Quakers should respond to the larger world around them. Were Quakers a part of this world but not of this world? Just how would Quaker beliefs fit within the context of the newly christened United States of America? Themes such as these would be routinely debated in Quaker meeting houses all across the land for many years to come.

Chapter 7: A Time of Great Adjustment

I believe there is something in the mind, or in the heart, that shows its approbation when we do right. I give myself this advice: Do not fear truth, let it be so contrary to inclination and feeling. Never give up the search after it; and let me take courage, and try from the bottom of my heart to do that which I believe truth dictates,
if it leads me to be a Quaker or not.

-Elizabeth Fry

By 1800, the Quakers were a strong, unified force that had spread across the nascent United States. This expansion continued as the United States gained territory farther west. In particular, the Quakers established enclaves in the newly established states of Ohio and Indiana, where slavery was illegal. Of course, this better suited the Quakers' sensibilities since they were completely against the abhorrent practice.

One of these enclaves was in Henry County, Indiana. By the year 1828, the Quakers had been in Henry County for about ten years. Here, they established a regular meeting organization known as the "Duck Creek Friends." The matters discussed among this group primarily pertained to the church. There were frank discussions of doctrine, as well as internal matters that needed to be hammered out, such as wayward Quakers who had broken the rules.

Although this was just one microcosm of Quakerism, the Duck Creek Friends of Henry County, Indiana, were fairly typical of what the Quaker experience was like during this period. At this point, the Quakers still firmly believed in a set of universal truths that every Quaker was expected to follow. The two main focal points for instruction were still Philadelphia and London, but the Quakers looked more to their own local leaders than to anyone else.

One of the great controversies to erupt during this period came from a Quaker minister from Long Island, New York, by the name of Elias Hicks. Hicks was a devout Quaker, but some of his beliefs differed from the traditional Quaker faithful. In particular, Hicks was assailed as having denied the "divinity of Christ." This criticism came from arguments Hicks had made in which he theorized that Christ was not born divine. Instead, Hicks believed he had become divine by living a sinless life and that he was in tune with the "Divine Light that was within him."

Again, one has to realize that the Quaker belief in which everyone has a "divine spark" or manifestation of God within them seems to verge on pantheism at times. Hicks apparently took this idea a step further by saying that Christ was no different than anyone else; he was just someone who suddenly woke up and realized that this spark—this manifestation of God—was within him and was then able to utilize it to its utmost perfection.

The implication that Hicks suggested was that anyone could emulate Christ if they simply chose to do so. This went against the doctrines of most Christian denominations, which clearly stress that all "fall short of the glory of God" and all need Christ as their intermediary in order to be saved.

Interestingly enough, even though Hicks seems to portray Christ as an ordinary figure who suddenly woke up to realize nirvana, he didn't deny all of the superhuman feats attributed to Christ. For example, even though Hicks downplayed the idea that Christ was born divine, he did not downplay the doctrine of the virgin birth. Hicks accepted that Christ had been born of a virgin, and basically every other miracle attributed to Christ, Hicks wholeheartedly believed. All the same, he still held fast to his theory that Christ's divinity was not achieved at birth but had manifested later in his life.

While some were drawn by Hicks's unique teachings, the traditional Quakers were disgusted by them, and they sought to end any further mention of what they viewed to be outright heresy being preached among their ranks. Those who were distressed by Hicks and his so-called "Hicksites" eventually found powerful backers in England, who came to visit the states in the 1820s. In this contentious debate, those who positioned themselves to be against Hicks came to be known as the "Orthodox Friends."

Hicks, however, was quick to point out the so-called "Orthodox Friends" were often more interested in "political power" and "material gain" than anything else. Those in the Orthodox faction insisted that the thing they were most interested in was simply sticking to the same doctrinal truths that most Christians held dear, namely that Christ was perfect from the beginning, as he was born the son of God, and that he was placed in this world for the sole mission of saving us by paying the price of human sin through his crucifixion.

However, the Orthodox Friends seemed to agree with Elias on his view that the scripture itself should not be elevated above the light of God. For Elias and apparently many other Quakers, the scriptures were viewed as a tool. But at the same time, the Orthodox Friends felt that Elias's teachings were dangerous because he veered too close to actually "diminishing" the Bible in a way that wouldn't be proper.

The friction between Elias, his supporters, and the more traditionalist Quakers would continue throughout much of the 1820s. This split seemed to also often fall along city and country lines. Most of the Quakers who lived in the cities often followed the Orthodox beliefs, whereas the rural, more remote Quakers were more likely to gravitate to Hicks's unorthodox teachings. The more urbane Quakers of Philadelphia, for example, often looked down their noses at the "prattling" teachings of Elias Hicks.

Hicks often ran afoul of the Orthodox Philadelphia leadership, no more so than Samuel Bettle and Jonathan Evans. Evans would become a common foil to Elias Hicks whenever he came to Philadelphia to preach. There were several noted instances in 1826 in which Hicks spoke at Quaker meeting houses in Philadelphia and was roundly rebuffed by Jonathan Evans. Every time Hicks would speak his peace in the meeting house, Jonathan would offer the Orthodox counterargument.

It was around this time that the so-called Hicksite/Orthodox separation became the most evident. The Hicksites were increasingly at odds with the world around them and called for reform, whereas the Orthodox were comfortable with business as usual and sought to maintain the status quo. It was in this fight that Hicks became an unlikely champion of reform. He was an obscure farmer, who used rural speech to get country Quakers interested in his ideas. But for many, his reforms weren't really new practices, as they were merely a call to get back to the Quaker roots that many felt had been lost.

In that sense, you could almost call the Hicksites throwbacks and conservatives to an earlier Quaker era. Along with this harkening back to the past, the Hicksites were also quite notorious for eschewing many modern conveniences. Hicks was known, for example, to speak out against the railroads, canals, and turnpikes, among other things. He even once criticized the building of Pennsylvania's Erie Canal by flatly stating, "If the Lord had intended there to be internal waterways, he would have placed them there."

But probably the thing that set the Hicksites and the urban Orthodox apart the most was Hicks's general disdain for city life. He viewed cities where people crowded around together as inherently corrupt and "centers of worldliness" and "lazy luxury." Or as he himself once put it, "What a vast portion of the joys and comforts of life do the idle and slothful deprive themselves of, by running into cities and towns to avoid laboring in the field."

Things would come to the point of no return in 1827 during the Philadelphia Yearly Meeting. Several Hicksites were determined to break away from the Orthodox hegemony of Philadelphia and form a yearly meeting of their own. And this was no small move. About "two-thirds" of the original membership actually left to join up with this new yearly meeting, creating two focal points of Quakerism right next to each other. This would lead to a domino effect, in which other meeting houses in places such as Baltimore and New York would follow suit, with the Hicksites separating themselves with their own meeting houses. As this veritable civil war between Hicksites and Orthodox Quakers erupted, the ideological lines between the two were starkly drawn.

But although the lines between the Orthodox and Hicksite Quakers were clear, the ranks of the Hicksites themselves were soon blurred and then fractured into several other groupings. The most numerous of these factions was one that could be considered to be conservative in its leanings, and they held the opinion that the Orthodox Friends had strayed away from the true path of Quakerism. Another strain rejected some of the ideas of Hicks and was instead more in step with the Orthodox Quakers. A third group was more liberal and actively involved in movements that were "radical" at the time, such as antislavery and women's rights. They were also keen on religious ideas outside of the Quaker faith, such as Unitarianism. The Unitarians were part of an early Christian movement that denied the Trinity and promoted the idea that God was one person.

Part of the reason the Hicksites fractured so early on could be attributed to outside pressure from society. For example, women's rights and the abolition of slavery were picking up steam, and Quaker activism in these two areas would lead to a refinement of many core Quaker beliefs.

Lucretia Mott was a Hicksite Quaker who played an integral role in the first summit for women's rights, which was held at Seneca Falls, New York, in the summer of 1848. Another social movement that attracted many Hicksites during this period was the American Anti-Slavery Society, which was formed in Philadelphia in December of 1833. Much as the name implies, this was an abolition group dedicated to the eradication of slavery, and it was the Quakers who led the charge.

Another focal point of activism/idealism that took hold of the Quakers during this period was that of the so-called "nonresistant movement." Quakers had long been against violence, and for those who considered themselves "nonresistors," the end goal was to create a society in which no coercive force was necessary.

This led to much experimentation in the 1840s with utopian-styled communities, which, in many ways, reflected upon William Penn's "holy experiment" with Pennsylvania about 200 years prior. Just like Pennsylvania under William Penn, the nonresistors attempted to create a society in which people could live in peace and harmony, without any military, police, or other coercive agent dictating how people should live.

The idea that humanity could live together without coercive measures in place to make sure citizens follow the rules has floated around for thousands of years. As recently as 2020, advocacy groups have tinkered with the notion that citizens can live without police enforcing the laws and have called for police departments to be defunded or perhaps even abolished outright. But such plans rarely—if ever—succeed.

Nevertheless, for these Quaker communes, the goal was to simply live a life based on the tenets of the New Testament and trust the other Quakers who participated in this experiment to keep themselves within the bounds of common decency, meaning no outside coercion was necessary. These nonresistor settlements began to pop up all over the place throughout the 1840s. As one can see, the first half of the

19th century proved to be a time of much experimentation and adjustment for the Quakers.

Chapter 8: The Quakers the Civil War and Its Aftermath

But in the central innermost region of our minds there shines one pure ray of direct light from the very throne of God. One ray which belongs to each one individually; which is for that one supreme and apart. The ray which shining from the heavenward side of conscience, and so enlightening and purifying, it must of necessity dominate the whole being.

–Carline Stephen

The Quakers were arguably one of the most proactive advocates for the end of slavery in the lead-up to the American Civil War. Along with advocating for the abolition of slavery, the Quakers were also quite busy during this period championing the cause for equality between the sexes, fair treatment of Native Americans, and the establishment of humane jail systems for prisoners, among other things.

Having said that, however, as forward-thinking as most Quakers may have been, they were a complicated group, and they were not always uniform in their march for justice. As mentioned previously in this book, not all Quakers supported freeing the slaves; in fact, some may have been direct beneficiaries from the enterprise. And even if

Quakers weren't involved in the slave trade, many merely rendered lip service during discussions on abolition.

At the same time, there were some deeply sincere abolitionists among the Quakers who would eventually leave the Quaker faith to more effectively pursue abolition. This segment of the Quakers often felt torn when it came to what they felt was expedient for religion and what they knew was most expedient for the social justice issues of the day.

A Quaker by the name of Amy Kirby Post found herself in just such a position. Kirby hailed from Long Island and grew up hearing all of the rumblings of Elias Hicks and the Hicksites. She became a regular at Hicksite gatherings by the late 1820s and would remain so over the next couple of decades. In the 1840s, however, she began to pull back from the Hicksites, who shunned the world, and she began to take a bold stand against what she saw as the evils of humanity.

Post still believed in core Quaker principles; she just sought to channel them into a more activist approach when it came to righting society's wrongs. This formula would lead Post to help form an offshoot of the Society of Friends, known as the Congregational Friends, which was formed in 1848. This group would then morph into the Progressive Friends before finally moving on to become the Friends of Human Progress.

Those involved in this organization were fully focused on racial and gender equality throughout the 1850s, leading right up to the American Civil War, which began in 1861. Amy Post was an interesting character. Although she was considered a progressive Quaker, she also had a deeply spiritual side to her, which can be seen in what were essentially "seances," which were conducted at her residence in Rochester, New York.

At first glance, the Quaker faith and the spiritualism movement may seem like strange bedfellows, but the ideologies merged among certain Quaker circles. After all, both the Quakers and the spiritualists gathered together in meetings in which they would sit in silence until supernatural forces moved them to speak, write, sing, or otherwise act. Of course, the big difference was that the Quakers believed they were being prompted by the spirit of God, whereas the spiritualists thought they were channeling disembodied spirits.

At any rate, Amy Post was just as dedicated to forging her own path in the spirit world as she was to finding justice in the physical realm. It seems that for a Quaker like Post, the Society of Friends only went so far when it came to righting America's wrongs, leading her to embrace more progressive blends of belief and activism. On the other hand, more traditional Quakers thought she had taken things further than she should have. At one point, the local meeting house she attended in Rochester, New York, actually chastised her for being "too worldly" due to her active involvement in the abolition movement. Worldly or not, Post pushed on.

One of the most effective ways she created change was to become involved in a little something called the Underground Railroad. The Underground Railroad was a clandestine route that slaves took when seeking to escape Southern plantations to the freedom of the north. The Underground Railroad actually had nothing to do with trains and railroads; it was simply an overland route that slaves were directed to take on their journey north. On this route were "stations," at which the slaves would stop at.

These "stations" were actually secretly designated safe houses, where abolitionists would take in the runaway slaves and give them food, shelter, and supplies before they headed back out onto their journey north. Amy Post and her husband, Isaac, maintained a station on the Underground Railroad and personally sheltered many slaves during their exodus to freedom. Another Quaker who was famous for conducting runaway slaves north during this period was Levi Coffin, whose home in Newport, Indiana, was an important stop on the Underground Railroad.

Coffin was such an integral figure of the Underground Railroad that he was sometimes known as the "President of the Underground

Railroad." Coffin himself estimated that he helped steward about one hundred slaves a year during his station's operation on the railroad. He was also noted for his cordial relationship with the freed African American community that lived in and around Newport. Coffin would regularly consult and organize efforts to aid further runaway slaves with this community. He treated his freed black neighbors as his friends and made them a part of his operations.

Sadly, Coffin was an exception rather than the rule. Many of the Quakers, even those who participated in the abolition movement, viewed segregation as a necessary component of life. This could obviously be seen during Quaker services. If African Americans were allowed to attend, they were almost always placed in segregated pews, and these separate pews could be pretty sternly enforced, as one Quaker activist discovered after being chewed out by a Quaker pastor in Philadelphia simply for sitting in the "colored" section of the meeting house.

Nevertheless, despite such internal prejudices, the Quakers soundly rejected slavery as a whole. And by the 1850s, the rejection of slavery was just about universal among the Quakers. They held firm on this, even as the faith fractured into more and more sects, for it was around this time that the Orthodox Quakers split into what would become known as the Gurneyites and the Wilburites.

The source of this split was due to a British Quaker by the name of Joseph John Gurney. Gurney came from an affluent background and had strong familial ties to the Quaker faith; he even counted the Quaker leader Robert Barclay among his ancestors. Gurney was a great speaker and an excellent scholar, who was quite gifted at arguing the finer points of what it meant to be a Quaker. He was also a passionate abolitionist and energized the Quaker base on this front as well.

In addition to all of this, Gurney was an advocate for what was known as "unprogrammed worship." This referred to a worship service that didn't follow any particular routine or "program."

Members would simply arrive at the meeting house and do what the spirit moved them to do. Some would sing, some would pray, some would speak, but much of the time, they would just sit in silence and listen—listening for that still small voice they knew to be God's.

In 1837, John Gurney came to spread his message to the United States, gaining many followers in the process. And by 1840, he gained his largest critic, a Quaker pastor from Rhode Island, by the name of John Wilbur. As one might surmise, the followers of Wilbur would become known as the aforementioned Wilburites.

One of their chief complaints was the fact that Gurney and his followers depended heavily on scripture. It must be noted with some irony that these Orthodox Quakers were distressed that Gurney put so much emphasis on scripture, whereas a couple of decades prior, the Orthodox Quakers were mad at Hicks for doing just the opposite. The Wilburites, it seems, sought a happy medium of not placing too much emphasis on scripture yet not denying its importance outright, as Hicks seemed to be on the verge of doing.

At any rate, the Quakers were even more ideologically divided by the time of the 1860 presidential election—a contest in which Republican abolitionist politicians stood to gain from the Quaker vote. Even though the Quakers were divided over internal doctrine, they were at this point in virtually complete agreement that slavery needed to end. The subsequent election of Abraham Lincoln that November, who actively courted the Quaker vote, would lead to several slaveholding Southern states seceding from the Union.

Although the election of Lincoln triggered the Southern states to rebel, the lead-up to the Civil War had been decades in the making. And if one event precipitated the Civil War more than any other, it would have to be John Brown's daring—and some might say dastardly—raid on Harper's Ferry. John Brown was a radical abolitionist who believed that slavery had to be stomped out at any cost, even if it meant taking violent action.

Even before Brown launched his raid on Harper's Ferry, which would lead to several dead and wounded, he had already murdered at least five people in cold blood in Kansas, allegedly in retribution against harassment carried out against abolitionists there. Surprisingly enough, for a group that was against nonviolence, there quite a few members of the Society of Friends who not only approved of John Brown's actions but also applauded them.

Perhaps most notable were the remarks of Levi Coffin, a stalwart abolitionist and Quaker conductor of the Underground Railroad. At the time of the raid on Harper's Ferry, Coffin, stated his belief that the condemned killer, John Brown, had been "an instrument in the hands of the Almighty to commence the great work of deliverance of the oppressed." As long as they could sit on the sidelines, the Quakers supported people as radical as John Brown. If it meant putting a dent into slavery, many Friends were all for it.

However, once the Civil War broke out in earnest, the Quakers would face a stark decision when it came to their principles. Once the guns began to fire, the Northern Quakers were the ones being drafted into the Union Army to take on the Confederates in the South. In the state of Indiana alone, it is estimated that about 25 percent of Quakers enlisted to serve in the Union Army. This meant the Quakers had to decide whether to hold firm to their commitment to nonviolence or temporarily put their pacifism aside to partake in a fight that nearly all Quakers viewed as just.

For the first time in the religion's history, many Quaker leaders quietly allowed their young men to pick up arms and join the army. A Quaker named Daniel Wooton was among those who took up the charge. Wooten described the sentiment at the time, saying, "We all know the Bible says thou shalt not kill: but what are we to do with those persons that rebel against the law of our country? Did God sit down and let the Devil take the uppermost seat in heaven when he caused the rebellion there? No Sir!"

Quakers like Daniel Wooten were ready to fight, and they felt the cause was just enough that God would be on their side. This was an opinion that was seconded by the likes of Captain Benjamin Nields, a Quaker who directed the 1st Delaware Light Artillery unit, which had amongst its ranks several Quakers. But it was another Delaware brigade—the 4th Delaware—that would boast one of the most dedicated Quaker soldiers.

His name was Henry Gawthrop, and at the outbreak of the war, he signed on with the 4th Delaware Regiment Volunteer Infantry. This brigade was put into action by Union Colonel Arthur H. Grimshaw in 1862. By the spring of 1864, Henry Gawthrop and his company were sent out to the front lines. During his time with the 4th Delaware, Gawthrop had to directly come to grips with the horrors of war and what it meant to his Quaker faith.

After surviving an early skirmish, Henry wrote home to tell his family all of the details:

> We have been under fire on picket and in the trenches since 9 o'clock yesterday morning at which time we marched from our camp of night before and took possession of the 2nd line of works. We were fired on by sharpshooters but no one hurt except private Ruth, pioneer of Co H, who was wounded in the right breast. Towards evening the rebels opened on us from their batteries and we had our first experience of shelling, and I can say that it was about the hardest of my life. Heaven's artillery was playing at the same time and the rain pouring down. Later we were marched more by the right. As we advanced in line through the woods the rebels opened on us and we poured in a volley and rushed for the breast works we were to occupy. Our fire drew that of their artillery and sharpshooters. We passed a very miserable night without rest. A constant fire from the rebels across the woods, and the rain pouring down.

Here, Henry highlights the incessant dread of open battle. The enemy was camped out just "across the woods" from them and was intermittently firing through the rain. Despite the hardship, Henry still looks toward God, likening the thunder and lightning he heard in the distance to "Heaven's artillery."

Henry Gawthrop would go through quite a bit during his service for the Union. He would be injured several times and end up having one of his feet amputated. But even through all of this trauma, he was thankful that, to his knowledge, he still hadn't broken the cardinal rule. As far as he knew, he hadn't actually killed anyone.

Or as Henry himself described it:

> I had been in great danger—three times wounded, horse shot, a bullet through my blanket roll and from shots striking objects near me, in different engagements. These experiences gave me a dislike of firearms, and (after leaving the arm) an uneasy feeling when one was handled near me. Except firing at a mark or firing the novel breech loading guns already noted, I made no use of firearms. I believe I have never killed anything in my life larger than a rat and I am glad of this though, of course, I shared fully in the responsibility, as I did the parts assigned to me. I was quite a success as a target. There was rarely any personal feeling on my part against the rank and file of our opponents and I think it was the same with my comrades. Whenever opportunity offered on picket line, we established, as it is shown in this narrative, friendly relations, though it was a dangerous practice, as someone higher up might end the parley without due notice.

Quakers were supposed to shun and abhor war, and it seems the actual experience of armed conflict only made Gawthrop detest the practice all the more. It's hard to believe that none of the bullets he fired while serving in the Union killed anyone, but this is what Henry Gawthrop maintained. He went through all the motions and participated in the charges, yet his bullets never killed anything "larger than a rat." Perhaps this was a miracle in itself, as it allowed Henry to participate in the fighting and keep his conscience clean.

It may have worked for Henry, but others would hold firm to their nonviolent stance and seek a way around the general call to arms the Union had made.

Fortunately for those in the latter camp, President Abraham Lincoln was willing to accommodate conscientious objectors. Unlike during the American Revolutionary War, when Quakers were sometimes thrown in jail for their refusal to participate in the war effort, Lincoln acknowledged religious objections to fighting and made an exception for them. This is the first known instance of conscientious objectors being accepted during wartime.

Though not a Quaker, Lincoln sympathized with their views on equality, as they were views he shared. Lincoln valued the Quakers' abolitionist sentiment and their votes, for he knew that a heavy Quaker voting bloc in Pennsylvania had been crucial for him in winning the state during the election of 1860. Lincoln knew the Quakers placed a high standard on the freedoms he held dear.

Just prior to his inauguration as president of the United States in 1861, Lincoln cited the Declaration of Independence as his compass when it came to the inherent freedoms that belonged to any man. The Declaration of Independence declared that all men were created equal, although it took the Civil War for America to finally recognize that creed, and it took even longer for the creed to finally benefit all citizens. Lincoln stated he "never had a feeling politically that did not spring from the [Declaration of Independence], which gave liberty, not alone to the people of this great country, but hope to the world for all future time."

President-elect Lincoln, full of passion and conviction, then made an ominous prediction, declaring, "If this country cannot be saved without giving up that principle—I would rather be assassinated on this spot than to surrender to it." As history can attest, Lincoln indeed died for his principles when Southern radical John Wilkes Booth assassinated him in 1865.

The Civil War came to a close on April 9th, 1865, when Confederate General Robert E. Lee signed the Confederate Army's surrender to the presiding Union General, Ulysses S. Grant. Although this was the official end of the war, hostilities would certainly linger, as was so tragically evidenced when Abraham Lincoln was hit by an assassin's bullet just five days later on the evening of April 14th.

Lincoln, sustaining mortal injuries, would cling to life before finally passing on the morning of April 15th, 1865. Much of the nation was sent into a state of shock and mourning at the news, especially the Quakers. After all, it was through Lincoln that the Quakers had finally achieved the abolition of slavery, for which they had fought so long and hard.

The Quakers had been such staunch abolitionists for so long that once the end of slavery was achieved, many Quakers wondered where their advocacy should be placed next. It didn't take them long to find it. It was just a few years after the war, in 1869, that President Ulysses S. Grant commissioned a group of Hicksite Quakers to engage in "humanitarian work" with the Native Americans.

Francis T. King, a notable Quaker, also led efforts during the Reconstruction era, helping to build up the educational systems of North Carolina. It was King and the Baltimore Association that established public schools in the region for both recently freed African Americans and European American residents. It is said that Quaker schools like this were used as a template for many of the public schoolhouses across the country.

Laura Haviland was another Quaker of this time period who played a prominent role in aiding freed slaves. When newly freed slaves were rendered refugees due to the rescinded former promise of forty acres and a mule, they migrated up to Ohio, Indiana, and Illinois in search of food and shelter. Laura made sure that Quakers were there to meet them. In Illinois alone, she managed to aid tens of thousands of newly freed African Americans. Despite the fact they arrived penniless, most became completely self-sufficient after being given this little bit of help. Haviland also would go on to work at the Freedmen's Aid Bureau in Washington, DC, where she ran educational workshops for newly freed African Americans.

The nation changed much after the conclusion of the American Civil War, and the Quakers changed just about as much as everyone else. The war had the effect of shaking up the faith and causing Quaker leaders to reconsider what they previously believed to be an excommunicable infraction among their members.

This was due in large part to the many young Quaker men who had broken the cardinal rule of holding fast to nonviolence so they could fight in the war. Previously, such things would have led to their dismissal from the church, but after the war, most Quaker meeting houses welcomed the young men back with open arms and no questions asked. This seeming willingness to bend the rules would lead to a general relaxation of others.

Most notably, it became more acceptable for Quakers to marry outside of their faith; for the last two centuries, such a thing was sternly frowned upon. At this point, the Quakers, who for many years had been known for their "peculiarity," began to become a widely accepted member of the mainline Protestant denominations. As such, the old Quaker meeting houses began to look more and more like traditional Protestant churches. In the aftermath of the Civil War, the Quakers, who had typically belonged on the fringes of Christianity, began to enter into the modern organization by which the Friends are known today.

However, with the abolition of slavery, the Quakers had lost the main unifying factor that had bound all of the Quaker factions together. Now that abolition had finally been achieved, Quakers wishing to create social change would have to find new modes of doing so.

Chapter 9: Some Modern-Day Quaking in the Making

There is something of God in every man, let us affirm it more certainly than ever. But surrounded as we are by millions of new-made graves and with the voices of the hungry and the dispossessed in our ears, let us not easily accept the impious hope that the natural goodness of ourselves is sufficient stuff out of which to fashion a better world.

–Gilbert H. Kilpack

The first decade of the 20th century was perhaps one of the most active for the Quakers. During this time, you could see Wilburites, Hicksites, and Gurneyites all holding regular meetings in search of how they could bring unity to Quakerism at large. It was during this period that the Wilburites began to go by the name of Conservative Friends.

As the name might imply, this sect of Quakers was the most traditional. In 1913, this group proclaimed their "common doctrinal statement." They became known for their insistence of eschewing all "religious symbolism," such as communion and all forms of water baptisms. People mainly attended gatherings in rural meeting houses, but these began to decline in the next few decades and would never quite recover.

The Hicksite strain of Quakerism in the early 20th century dropped the name Hicksite in favor of the "Friends General Conference," or just "FGC" for short. Despite the rebranding, Hicksite membership began to decline. It is estimated that by 1900, the Hicksites had been reduced to a number of somewhere around 17,000 members. Such low membership was certainly not encouraging, and by 1919, the trend was even more pronounced, with attendance at meetings in Illinois, Indiana, and New York only reaching into the hundreds.

Around this time, a little-known town just north of Indianapolis, called "Westfield," became a Quaker hot spot of sorts. Nestled in the middle of cornfields and country roads, Westfield, Indiana, was the "Union Bible Seminary." This seminary became actively involved in overseas missions, and in 1919, it launched mission trips to the South American country of Bolivia.

However, a shift began to take place by the end of the 1920s, with larger Hicksite (FGC) gatherings emerging in major urban areas, such as Ithaca, New York, and Cleveland, Ohio. With these newly established urban centers, the FGC managed to even itself out over the next couple of decades. 1926 was an especially pivotal year for the FGC since a new charter was developed to foster "uniform discipline" among all their members.

The Gurneyites, on the other hand, were initially not very well-organized and continued to have trouble uniting their base. By the 20th century, much of this base actually centered around Richmond, Indiana. Eventually, they got their act together and would become great missionaries, taking the Quaker doctrine as far afield as Kenya, India, China, and even Alaska. Their work in Kenya would have the most lasting legacy. Kenya, to this day, has more Quakers than anywhere else outside of the United States.

In the 20th century, the Quakers almost universally stuck to their guns when it came to nonviolence, refusing to participate in either

World War One or World War Two if it meant they had to take another human being's life. This doesn't mean the Quakers weren't involved in the world wars. While some Quakers refused to aid in the war effort at all, as they were outright conscientious objectors who preferred to sit on the sidelines, other Quakers participated in the world wars in assisting roles, becoming medics or ambulance drivers. British Quakers streamlined this service even further by creating their own ambulance service, which they called the Friends' Ambulance Unit.

This worked well enough for most, but for those who considered themselves to be so-called "absolutist conscientious objectors," even participating in an ambulance service was going too far. According to the sentiments of these absolutist Quakers, war was an all or nothing enterprise, and you were either helping the war effort or were not. For them, driving an ambulance for the Allies was just as bad as picking up a gun since it was aiding in the overall war effort.

A Briton named Wilfrid Littleboy was one of these absolutist conscientious objectors. As soon as the war began, he held fast to his Quaker principles and refused to have any part in the war effort. He didn't know what would happen to him or what kind of punishment he might receive for shirking his marching orders, but he just couldn't bring himself to compromise all he held dear.

Initially, officials took a light-handed approach with Wilfrid, and in his first hearing, which was presided over by none other than future Prime Minister Neville Chamberlain, he was given a wide range of options as it pertained to non-combat roles. Wilfrid remembered Neville as being quite kind, considerate, and accommodating. The meeting ended with Neville Chamberlain simply asking Wilfrid to "think about it."

But at Wilfrid's second hearing, those who met with him were not quite so kind. Neville Chamberlain was gone, and in his place was a presiding officer who took on an adversarial tone from the very beginning. This man had neither the respect nor the patience to hear about Wilfrid's Quaker beliefs, and he instead lambasted the young man for failing to sign on to any of the non-combat roles that had been offered to him.

Wilfrid Littleboy was once again directed to sign on with the Non-Combatant Corps. Wilfrid, however, had no such intention of doing so. This wasn't a flippant decision on Wilfrid's part since he knew he could be apprehended and hauled off to jail for failing to report to duty. As Wilfrid described it, "One almost got used to the fact that you might go into town one day and be picked up without any warning."

That day came in 1916 when Wilfrid went to a Quaker meeting one night only to find the police camped out, waiting for him to leave. The police informed Wilfrid that he would have to report to court and answer for his evasion of service. He faithfully attended the hearing the next day and was then promptly placed into military custody.

The military authorities basically tried to force Wilfrid to enlist. They tossed a soldier's uniform at him and ordered him to put it on. Wilfrid refused, and in doing so, he was immediately court-martialed. He now went from Quaker conscientious objector to Quaker inmate, and he was sent to a military jail—all because he simply didn't want to take part in the war.

Wilfrid would remain incarcerated for the duration of the war. World War One came to a close on November 11th, 1918, but Wilfrid Littleboy would not be released until the following year, in 1919. Wilfrid didn't hold any grudges for his internment, and upon his release, he immediately got back to work and back to the Quaker meeting house. Wilfrid's experience was fairly typical of what many Quaker conscientious objectors went through during the war.

After the war was over, the Quakers showed they didn't take any sides when it came to the needy, as they immediately rendered their services to Germans who needed assistance just as they would to their own countrymen. While Germans struggled under a bankrupt and broken economy, the Quakers rushed forward to render aid through food supplies and whatever else they could muster.

World War Two would prove to be the most pivotal for the Quakers, as it brought those of the Quaker faith together from all over the globe, forging bonds that had been loose into a much tighter knot. It was this wartime solidarity that brought about the Friends World Committee for Consultation.

The Quakers during World War Two would render much-needed relief to both troops and civilians during the war. But the most heroic Quakers were behind enemy lines. In both Germany and Italy, Quakers were present on the ground helping to aid civilians, even under the threat of being arrested and sent to a concentration camp. Despite such terrible repercussions, the Quakers refused to stand idly by while others suffered.

In fact, the Quakers played a vital role in rescuing Jews from being sent to the death camps. In what was essentially an "underground railroad" in Western Europe, the Quakers created a series of safe houses that allowed them to conduct Jewish refugees to freedom, with many of their charges seeking asylum in America and Great Britain. These efforts led the Quaker branches of the American Friends Service Committee and the British Friends Service Council to receive a Nobel Peace Prize after the war.

As confusing as all of the Quakerism sects can be, it was shortly after World War Two that yet another brand of Quakerism hit the mainstream, which would become known as the Association of Evangelical Friends. This was founded in 1947.

That same year, a prominent Quaker named Clarence Picket announced at a conference of Quakers that the tensions between the Soviet Union and the US had become so dangerous that the Quakers should do what they could to stem the aggression. So, on the eve of the Cold War, the Quakers decided to become more politically involved than ever before.

In fact, it was under the auspices of this reenergized Quakerism that a young man by the name of Richard Nixon would come to prominence. Yes, not many are aware of it, but tricky Dick Nixon—the US president so often scorned for his actions at Watergate—was indeed a Quaker. Nixon began his life in Yorba Linda, California, where he grew up as a Quaker throughout the 1920s and 1930s. Nixon graduated from the Quaker-founded Whittier College in 1933. The school was named after a famous Quaker abolitionist by the name of John Greenleaf Whittier.

Vice President Richard Nixon discussed the sad state of America's race relations in the 1950s with Martin Luther King Jr., lamenting how racial disparities at home were absolutely devastating for the nation's reputation abroad. How could the US tout itself as the leader of the free world and a better alternative to communist Russia if everyone in America were not being accorded the same rights?

Martin Luther King was apparently convinced of Nixon's sincerity, and he walked away with a favorable view of the Quaker politician. Martin Luther King later went on the record to state, "Nixon happens to be a Quaker and there are very few Quakers who are prejudice [sic] from a racial point of view."

Others would later contend that Nixon was simply a good actor and that he was often able to manipulate his conversations well enough to appear to be whatever anyone wanted at the time. And since the Republicans of the 1950s were actively supportive of the nascent civil rights movement, some would say that Nixon was simply trying to play that angle up for all it was worth. But nevertheless, when Nixon spoke of his Quaker values when it came to equality, Martin Luther King believed him to be sincere.

And if anyone knew the Quakers, Martin Luther King Jr. did. King was actually very involved with Quaker organizations throughout the 1950s and 1960s. Martin Luther King's relationship with the Quakers dates back to 1955, the year that Rosa Parks famously "sat down for her rights" by refusing to stand when a white patron wanted her seat.

This event led to widespread bus boycotts in Montgomery, Alabama, which were led by King. The Quakers heard of these happenings and began to debate whether this was a social issue they should become involved in. In the spring of 1956, the civil rights movement was a matter of intense discussion at the Philadelphia Yearly Meeting.

The Quakers were finally moved to action after the secretary of the "Yearly Meeting Peace Committee" spoke with King on the phone, who agreed to send a group of Quakers to Alabama. These Quakers worked like a fact-finding mission to determine just what was happening on the ground. They soon saw firsthand the oppression African Americans were facing. At the same time, they were greatly impressed by the skillful, nonviolent resistance Martin Luther King Jr. led.

Around the time Nixon first ran for president in 1960, the Quakers saw their next major surge in growth, which would lead to the formation of the Evangelical Friends Alliance. This movement would lead to the founding of several more churches in places like Nixon's Yorba Linda, California, as well as Ohio, Virginia, North Carolina, and Florida.

As action heated up in a little-known place called Vietnam in the 1960s, the Quakers entered into a new and decisive phase of activism, in which they dared to defy their own government in order to help the Vietnamese. The Vietnam War was a complicated affair from the very beginning. Vietnam had previously been a French colony, but after the French had been shaken loose by the Japanese during World War Two, the Vietnamese sought to establish their own independence.

However, the French weren't quite willing to relinquish their possession and sought to regain control. In their struggle, the Vietnamese made the mistake of embracing communist ideology as the avenue for their deliverance. This provoked the ire of the United States government, which was increasingly wary of the spread of communism during the Cold War. So, after the bloodied and beat French gave up and pulled out of Vietnam, the United States stepped right in, in order to prevent a communist takeover of Southeast Asia.

The US backed a pro-capitalist government in South Vietnam and actively aided them in their fight against the communists of North Vietnam. When the South Vietnamese were on the verge of defeat, the Americans put their thumb on the scale and decided to intervene directly. This war, fought on the basis of correcting the ideology of a foreign land, led to tragic outcomes in regard to civilian death and destruction, as American warplanes began to hammer the North Vietnamese and US troops burned down villages, seeking to put a stop to the communist advance.

This carnage inspired the Quakers to go against their own country and aid average Vietnamese civilians on the ground. The Society of Friends mailed "relief packages" to North Vietnam in 1966. However, these efforts were halted by the post office, which refused to deliver aid to an enemy combatant of the United States. The Quakers also attempted to send aid in the form of cold hard cash through the Red Cross Society located in North Vietnam, but this, too, was seized by US government officials before the North Vietnamese could use it.

If that wasn't enough to make sure those troublesome Quakers knew the federal government meant business, the Friends were then threatened with a possible ten-year prison sentence from an old bit of legislation from 1917 called the "Trading with the Enemy Act." The act grants the authority to an American president to prosecute anyone conducting any kind of trade with enemies of the United States.

It wouldn't be the first time that Quakers were viewed as enemies and potential communist collaborators. When Richard Nixon was vice president of the United States in the 1950s under the Eisenhower administration, he alerted his associates that he believed communists were manipulating the sympathies of Quaker groups. Although Richard Nixon himself was a Quaker, he was ready to lay down the gauntlet against them in spite of his beliefs.

Nevertheless, even with the threat of jail time, the Quakers weren't willing to simply give up, and in 1967, the Quaker Action Group took the audacious step of sending a yacht loaded with supplies to North Vietnam. On March 22nd, 1967, the yacht left, and it would ride the waves for five days from a Quaker enclave in Hong Kong to enemy territory in North Vietnam.

The captain, an anthropologist and explorer by the name of Earle L. Reynolds, suggested they should be armed in case they got into trouble. The Quakers, of course, refused, citing their nonviolent beliefs. For this trip, they weren't going to put their faith in guns; they were going to put all of their faith in God. And they would need it. Because as soon as they docked in the Gulf of Tonkin, they were greeted with a volley of artillery fire.

This burst of artillery was not meant for them, though; it was for those who were lurking in the skies above. Soon after, they would discover that an American fighter craft had just been shot down. Most Americans wouldn't appreciate the fact that Quakers were aiding the North Vietnamese—especially since they were aiding them while they were in the process of killing Americans—but the Quakers were indeed a rarified bunch. Due to their wide-ranging views of morality, they felt the North Vietnamese needed their help, and they would do so whether anyone else agreed with them or not.

The Quakers were indeed well received by the North Vietnamese, who were grateful for the medical supplies as well as the kind gesture it represented. They gave the Quakers a grand tour of their stomping grounds, taking them to lavish banquets that had been prepared in their honor, as well as having them visit the sick and injured Vietnamese in their hospitals. By the time word of this reached the American press, the reactions were understandably mixed and matched the polarized sentiment of the time.

By the late 1960s, about half of the American public was against the war, while the rest still deemed it a necessary struggle against the creeping advance of communism. Those who were against the war, predictably enough, applauded the Quakers' efforts. In contrast, those who supported the struggle against the communist North Vietnamese deemed the Quakers' aiding of enemy combatants a travesty and an outright betrayal of all the blood America lost fighting them.

The Quakers just wanted to help people, and to show they were not taking a side in the conflict, they sent supplies to South Vietnam on their next voyage. However, the South Vietnamese didn't want anything to do with them and refused to let the boat land. At one point, they even threatened the Quakers with artillery. The Quakers were finally forced to sail to Hong Kong and have some of the supplies shipped through anonymous freight.

The Quakers then made their final trip to Vietnam in January 1968, this time returning to North Vietnam. They were indeed successful in once again dropping off medical aid packages, but due to the ramping up of the Tet Offensive, they had to make a quick getaway lest the Americans "bomb the port to ashes." Predictably, those who were against the Vietnam War supported the Quakers' efforts, and those who were for it were aghast, calling them unpatriotic at best and downright traitors at worse.

In the 1970s, the Society of Friends would wade into perhaps even more tumultuous, polarized political waters when they weighed in on the Israeli/Palestinian conflict. Seemingly siding with the Palestinians, the Quakers demanded that all US aid to Israel cease at once. In 1973, during the Yom Kippur War, the Quakers pushed for the United States to enter into an arms embargo with Israel. The US, of course, wasn't about to do any such thing.

The Quakers were persistent and decided to take matters into their own hands. They opened up shop right in Israel and began to send Quaker counsel to any Palestinians standing trial in Israeli courtrooms. The Quakers continued their activism throughout the 1980s, regularly taking a stand against such things as nuclear proliferation and South Africa's apartheid, just to name a couple of the Quaker movements at work.

They had the most grassroots success in South Africa. In the 1980s, during the height of the resistance to apartheid, the Quakers founded their Peace Centre in Cape Town in order to take in refugees who had been expelled by the apartheid regime. The Friends also rendered much-needed monetary assistance to apartheid activist Steve Biko's Black Communities Programmes, as well as Winnie Mandela's home industries for black women.

The most arguably influential Quaker in the struggle against apartheid in South Africa was Nozizwe Madlala-Routledge. Nozizwe ceaselessly led protests for the end of apartheid all throughout the 1980s, ending up in jail for her efforts. Nevertheless, she would rise above the adversity and become an active participant in the ending of apartheid. In 1999 when Nelson Mandela was president, Nozizwe was made deputy minister of defense. In this role, Nozizwe took on the task of spreading awareness on South Africa's greatest enemy at the time—AIDS. She spearheaded a movement to bring the epidemic to the public's awareness.

Meanwhile, Quakers in the United States were busy with relief efforts throughout all kinds of catastrophes and incidents of civil unrest, from the Los Angeles riots of 1992 to Hurricane Katrina in 2005. Their relief efforts during Katrina were particularly memorable, with Quakers literally sending out truckloads of food and other much-needed supplies to aid the hurricane survivors. Leading this charge was the Friends Disaster Service (FDS). The FDS was founded in 1974 after a tornado struck the Quaker-friendly town of Xenia, Ohio. During Hurricane Katrina, the FDS was crucial when it came to helping those who weren't able to help themselves.

The FDS was again on the scene when a major earthquake hit Haiti. There, they not only supplied food and medical supplies but also played an active role in rebuilding much of the devastated infrastructure. Perhaps their greatest relief effort is still unfolding. Since the COVID-19 pandemic erupted in the spring of 2020, the Quakers have been on the frontlines, helping to fight this terrible scourge of humanity. The Quakers have been instrumental in their efforts to send food, supplies, and personal protection equipment to areas hit hard by the coronavirus. They also raised substantial funds to help out those facing eviction or in need of a little bail money to get out of overcrowded COVID-19 infested jails.

Whatever and wherever they thought they could make a difference, the Quakers have always done their best to make the world a better place. The jury is still out on whether they were always on the right side of history, but the Quakers have at least made an effort to maintain William Penn's original vision. "Right is right, even if everyone is against, and wrong is wrong even if everyone is for it."

William Penn was a man who was shaped by his revelatory experiences, and he knew that the divine love he experienced, if harnessed properly, could change the world. If we would just utilize the divine light—the innate good in all of us—we would never be led astray. As we harken back to the words of William Penn all those years ago, one can't help but feel that some modern-day quaking might yet still be in the making.

Conclusion: The State of Quakerism

History is full of religious sects that broke away from their main religious body in order to express new fundamental truths and insights to the masses. After all, Christianity was originally an offshoot of Judaism that proclaimed a new means of salvation was at hand. In a similar fashion, George Fox had a revelation of what it meant to be a Christian and how one should approach God. During the time of the first Quakers, the Church controlled much of the religious experience of worshipers, dictating when to arrive, where to sit, what to sing, and what to pray.

Prior to the Reformation, many were not even allowed to read the Bible for themselves, and they were forced to only hear scripture through the interpretation of their local priest or pastor. Martin Luther, the Reformation leader who rocked the Catholic Church in the early 1600s, railed against the fact individuals were not allowed to seek God on their own terms but rather through the lens of the clergy.

The likes of George Fox and the Quakers took this much further, and they not only decided they didn't need a pope and a bunch of cardinals in distant Rome dictating their relationship with God, but they also didn't need religious finery, icons, or ceremonies. The

Quakers taught that each of us has the inner light of God inside of us, and in order to commune with Him, we don't need pieces of bread and grape juice—we just need to sit quietly and get in tune with the consciousness that resides inside.

As excited as the Quakers were about their perceived revelation, many were not too pleased with the notion that the Church or even the Bible might not be necessary for salvation. Even Martin Luther himself might have objected to some of these teachings. Nevertheless, the Quakers believed they had stumbled upon a cosmic secret that few others had realized. They believed that the light of God could shine bright in humanity if they would only come to realize that God didn't dwell in churches made of stone but within human beings made of flesh.

Those who came to understand and appreciate this teaching often felt as if they had been struck by lightning at the realization. This was precisely how William Penn felt all those years ago when he heard a poor and humble old Quaker minister preach at his dad's castle. Upon hearing the words of Thomas Loe, William Penn felt as if he had just uncovered the greatest secret of the universe. God wasn't in some faraway dimension somewhere; he dwelled deep within our souls and could be tapped into at any time!

The concept the Quakers developed had far-reaching social ramifications. They came to realize that if everyone had the inner light of God within them, that must mean that everyone was equal in the eyes of God. This concept of equality was already backed up by scripture. After all, Apostle Paul famously declared, "For ye are all the children of God by faith in Christ Jesus. For as many of you as have been baptized into Christ have put on Christ. There is neither Jew nor Greek, there is neither bond nor free, there is neither male nor female: for ye are all one in Christ!"

This statement of equality comes right out of the New Testament, but for the Quakers, it was their revelatory experience with the divine light within that made the equality of God all the more real to them.

And once they came to believe it, it made them value all human life as precious. How could they harm someone who had the light of God dwelling within them? How could one look down upon, abuse, enslave, or otherwise mistreat a vessel that God works through? To them, it would be like maliciously burning down a church or tearing down an altar!

This understanding led the Quakers to refuse the recognition of ranks, titles, and distinctions. This great vision of equality guided the Quakers to treating others with respect. This could be seen early on, with the Quakers treating Native Americans with dignity and denouncing slavery centuries before most other Christians would even dare to approach the subject. The Quakers' strong convictions and beliefs made them stand out, and they were persecuted early on because of it.

As the trials and tribulations of a young William Penn can attest, even something as innocuous as not taking the hat off one's head could land a Quaker in jail. Nevertheless, they persisted, and the more they were persecuted, the more they persevered. So much so, that someone like Penn, who had spent time in the dreaded Tower of London, would later be commissioned to found the American Colony of Pennsylvania.

William Penn himself did not take this great reversal in fortune for granted. On the contrary, he made sure he remained humble and faithful to the tenets of Quakerism for the rest of his days, as he was determined to leave behind a legacy of Quaker values long after he passed from this earth. All one has to do is look at a copy of the US Constitution to find Penn's values of freedom of religion and freedom of speech since they are enshrined in the nation's Bill of Rights.

Most would say a Quaker like Penn was a true visionary, but William Penn would probably humbly admit that it was not his vision but God's that allowed him to fashion such an epic charter of human rights in the first place. This was indeed the state of Quakerism then, and as long as we hold fast to the great legacy and principles that

Quakers like William Penn left behind, it will continue to be the state of Quakerism for the foreseeable future.

Here's another book by Captivating History that you might be interested in

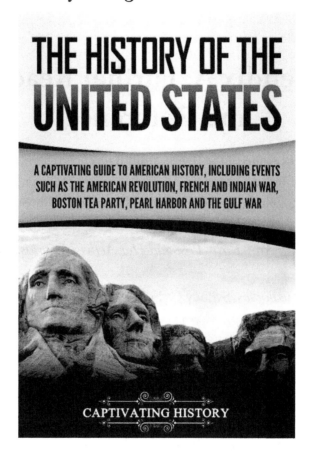

THE HISTORY OF THE UNITED STATES

A CAPTIVATING GUIDE TO AMERICAN HISTORY, INCLUDING EVENTS SUCH AS THE AMERICAN REVOLUTION, FRENCH AND INDIAN WAR, BOSTON TEA PARTY, PEARL HARBOR AND THE GULF WAR

CAPTIVATING HISTORY

Appendix A: Further Reading and Reference

Here is a list of some of the reading and reference materials that helped make this text possible. All of these sources cover a wide-ranging variety of the Quaker story. Feel free to look through them on your own.

Radical Friend: Amy Kirby Post and Her Activist Worlds. Nancy A. Hewitt

The Quaker Colonies. Sydney G. Fisher

A Quaker Officer in the Civil War: Henry Gawthrop of the 4th Delaware. Justin Carisio

Abraham Lincoln, the Quakers, and the Civil War: A Trial of Principle and Faith. William C. Kashatus

The Rich Heritage of Quakerism. Walter R. Williams

The Quakers in America. Thomas D. Hamm

The Light in Their Consciences: Early Quakers in Britain, 1646-1666. Rosemary Moore

The Quakers, 1656-1723: The Evolution of an Alternative Community. Richard C. Allen and Rosemary Moore

A Lenape Among the Quakers: The Life of Hannah Freeman. Dawn G. Marsh

Nixon's First Cover Up: The Religious Life of a Quaker President. H. Larry Ingle

The Worlds of William Penn. Andrew R. Murphy, John Smolenski

Made in the USA
Middletown, DE
20 December 2021

56749244R00056